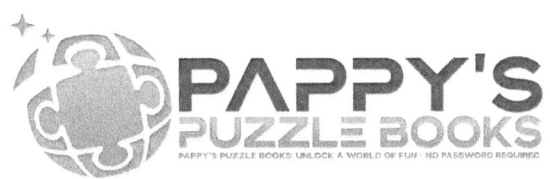

For additional Pappy's Puzzle Boo

Just scan the QR code or go to:

www.pappyspuzzlebooks.com

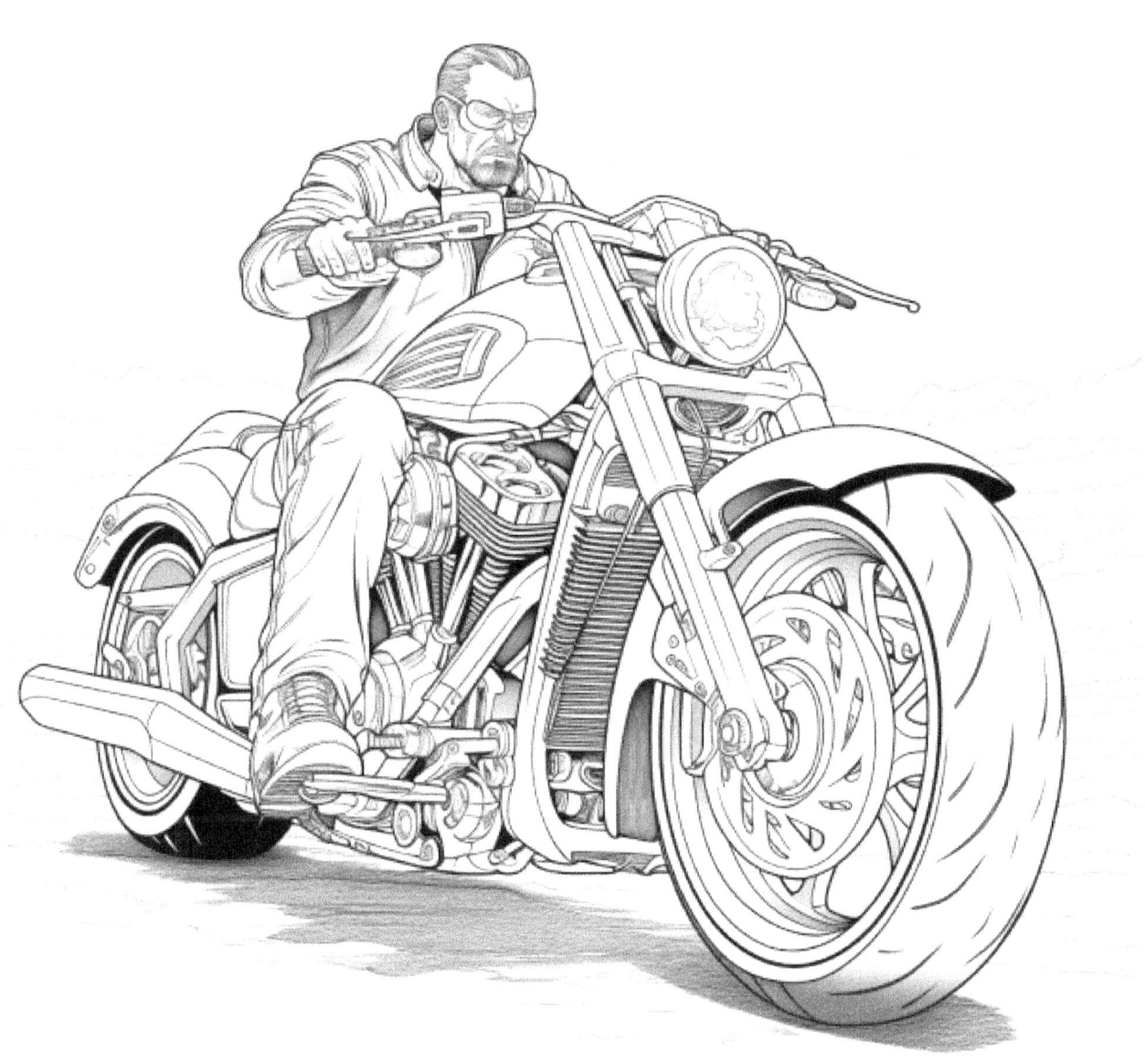

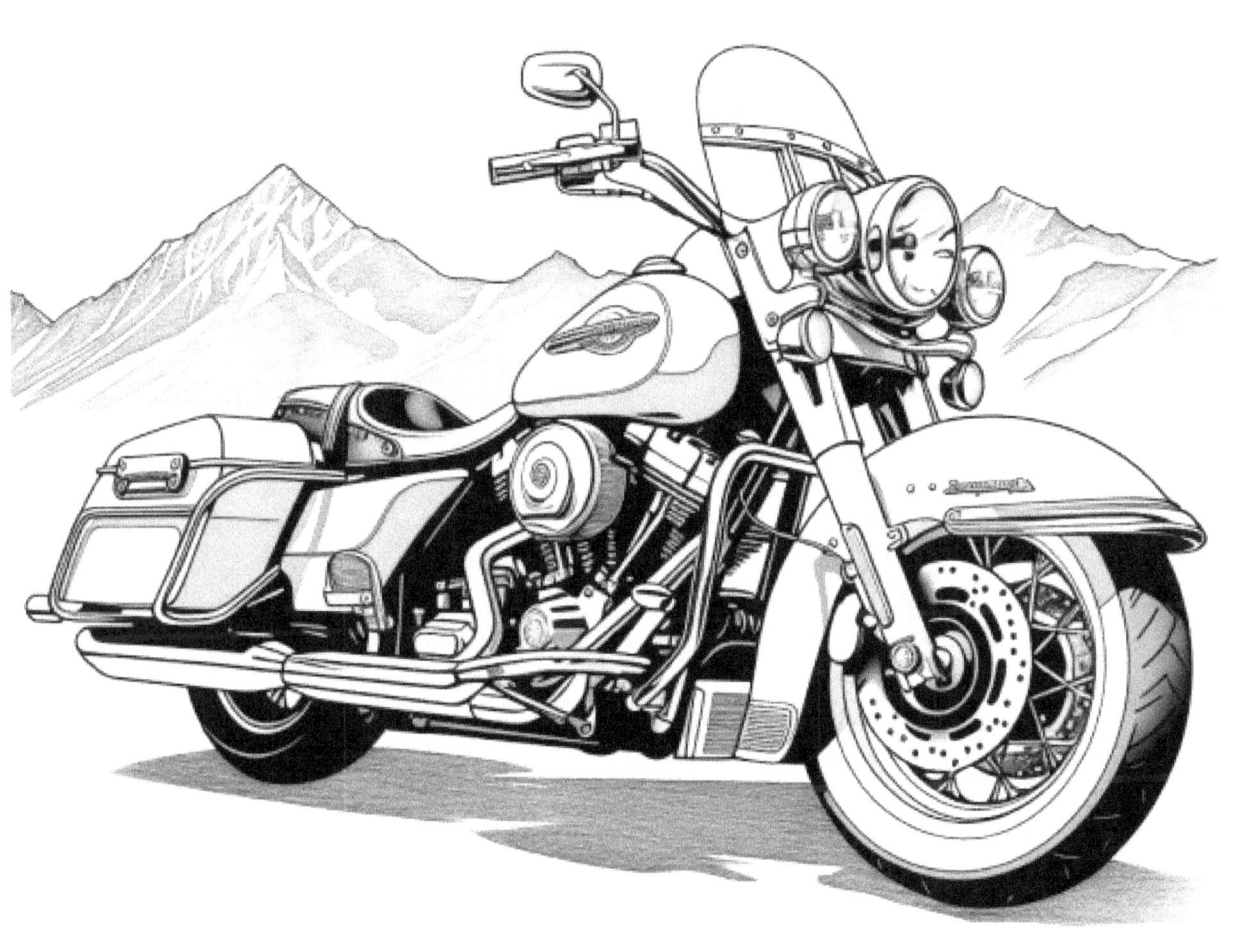

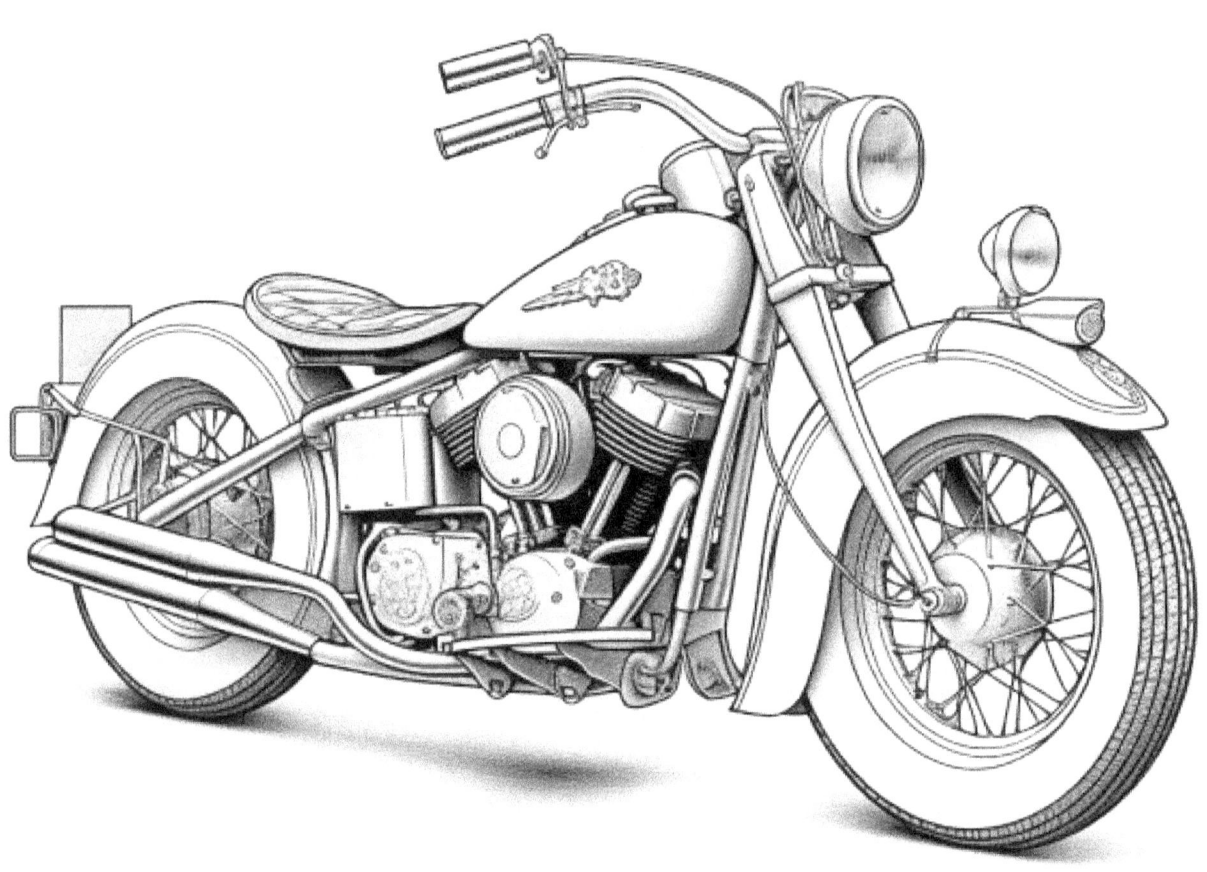

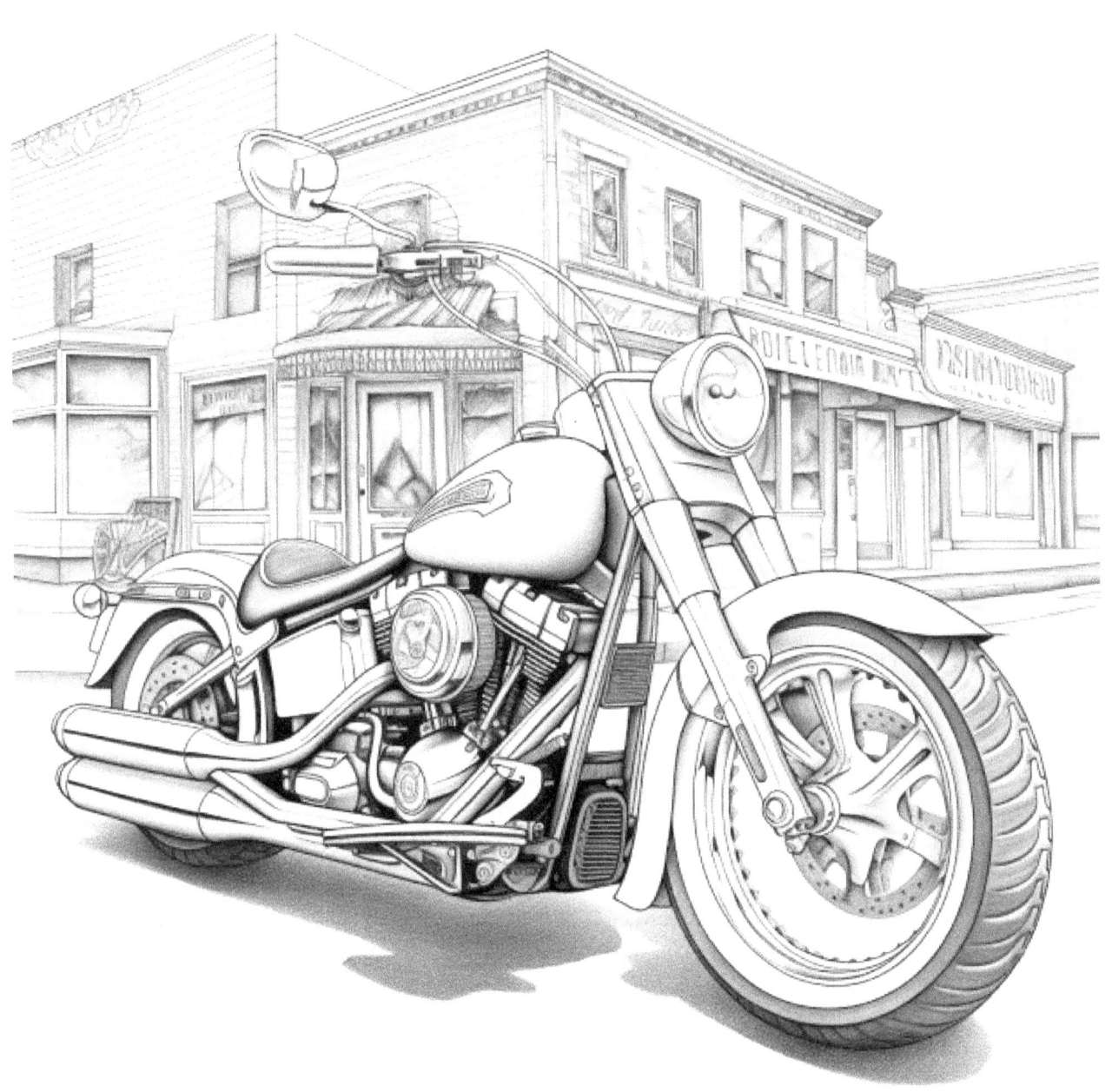

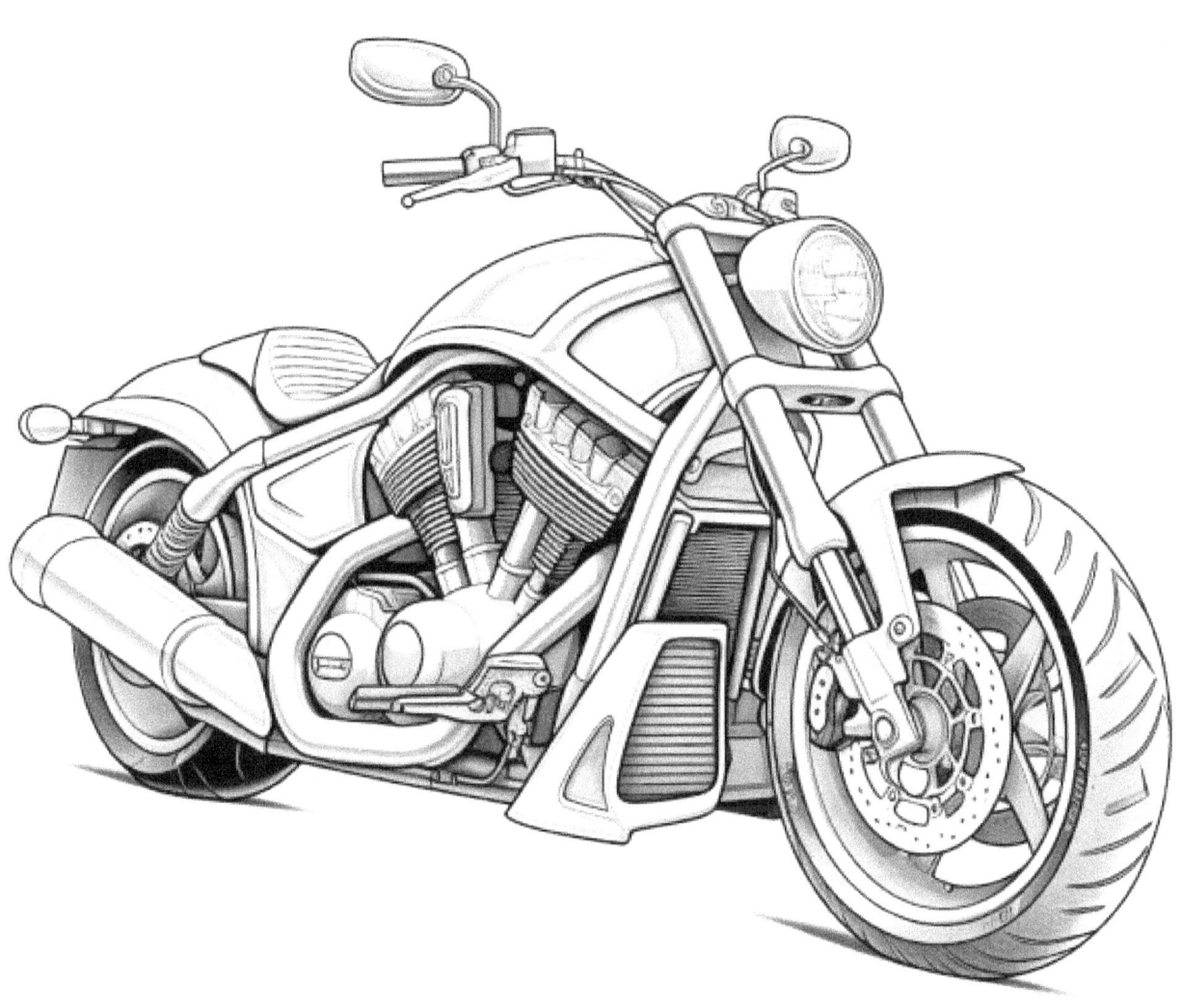

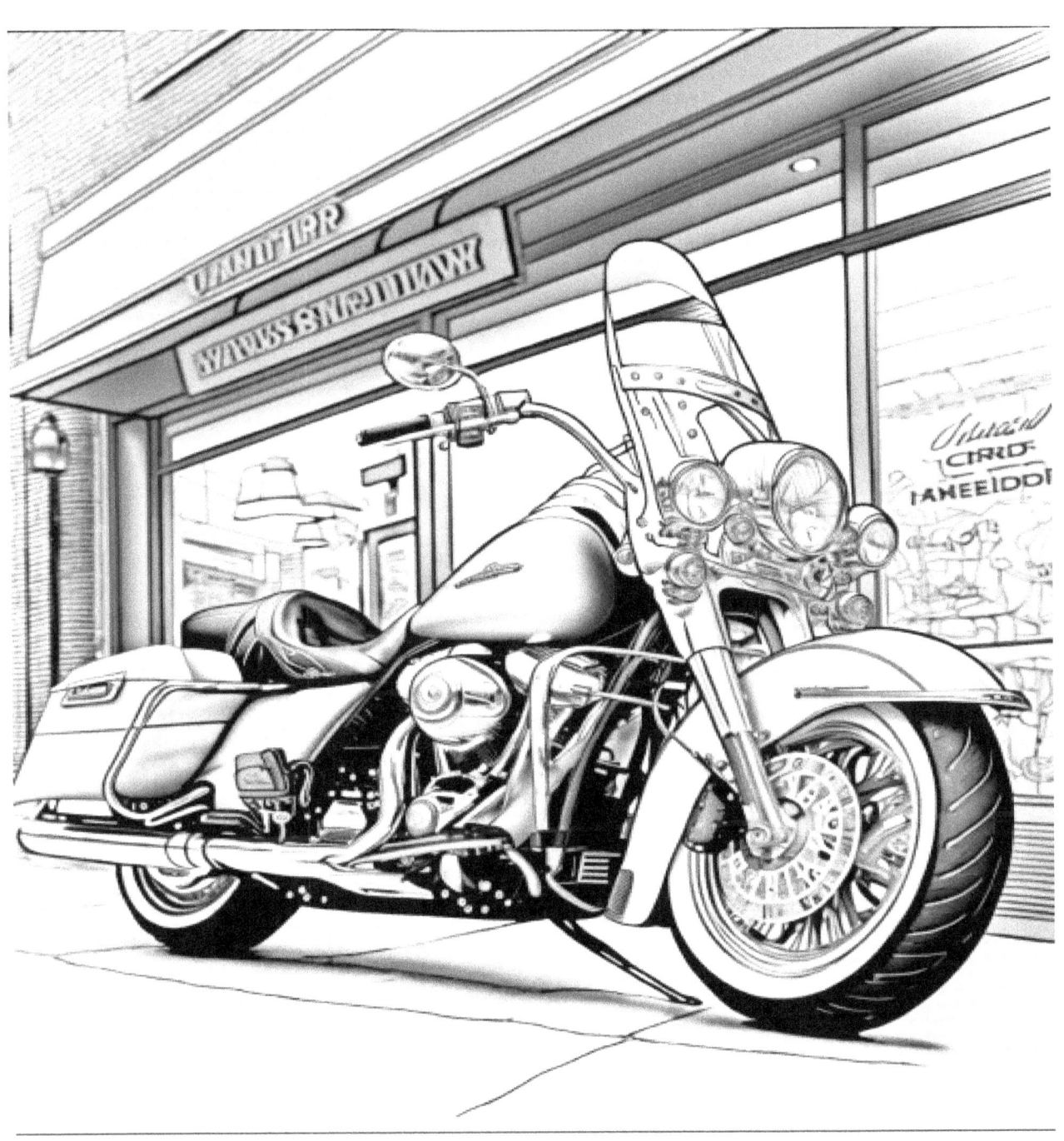

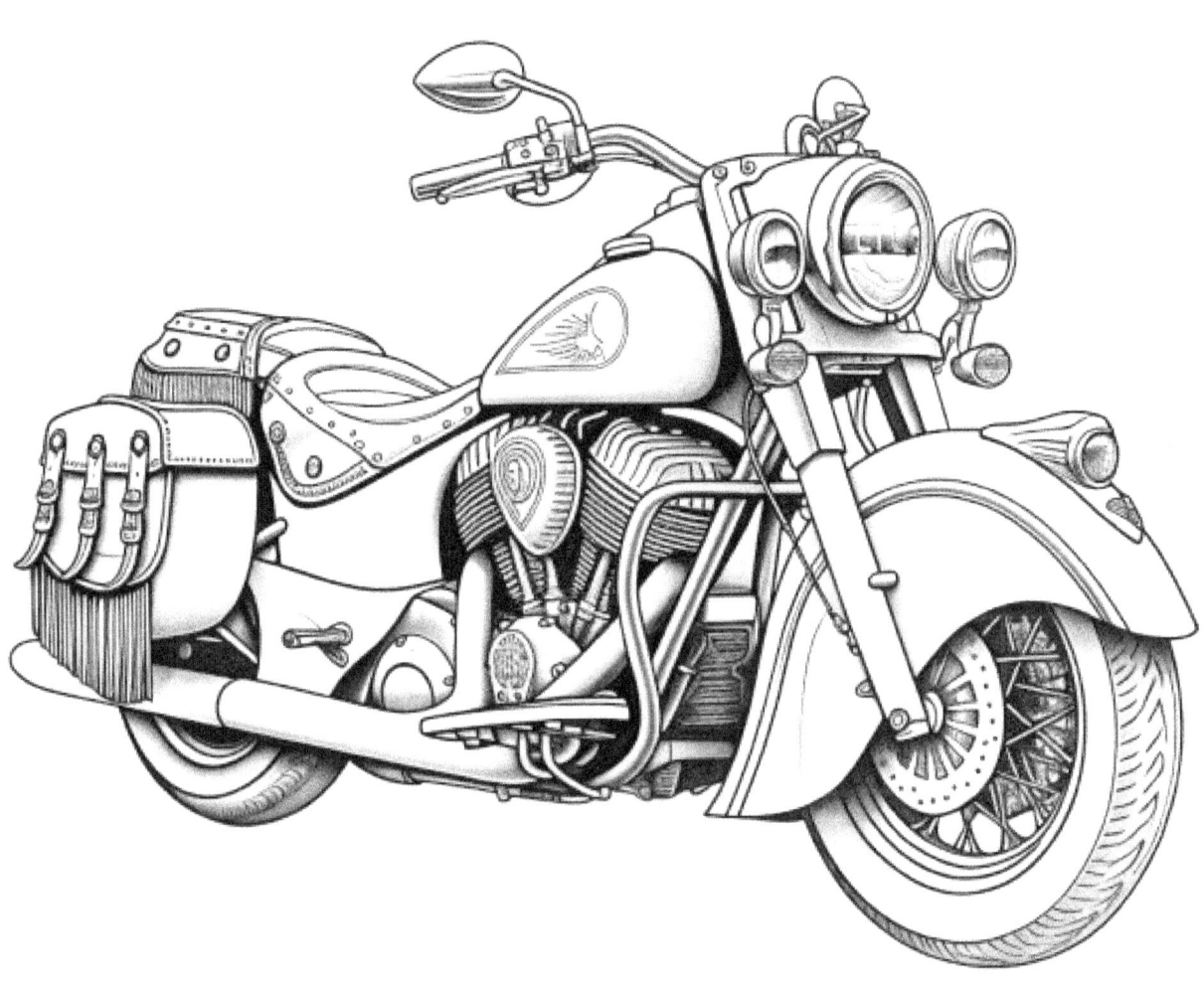

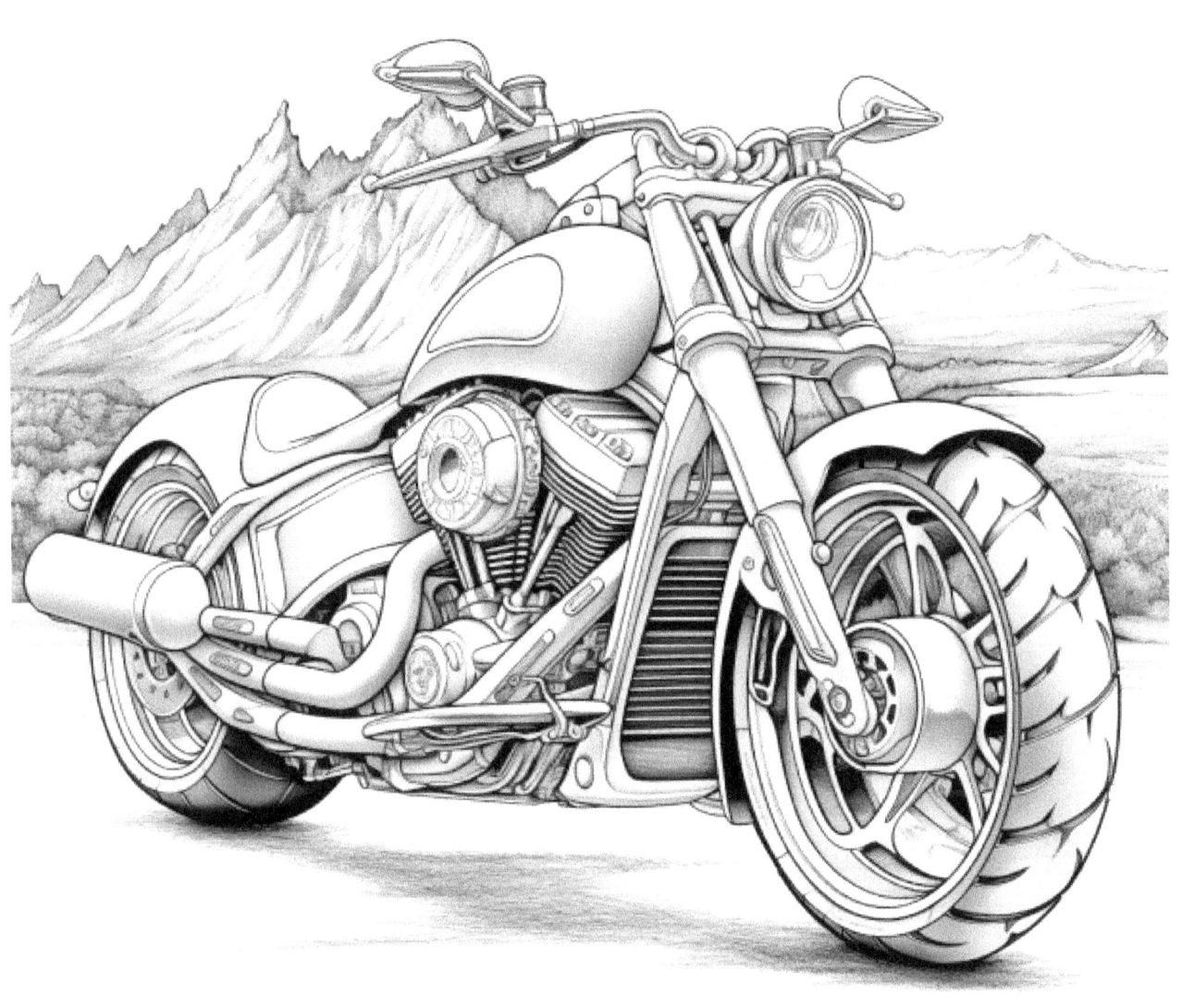

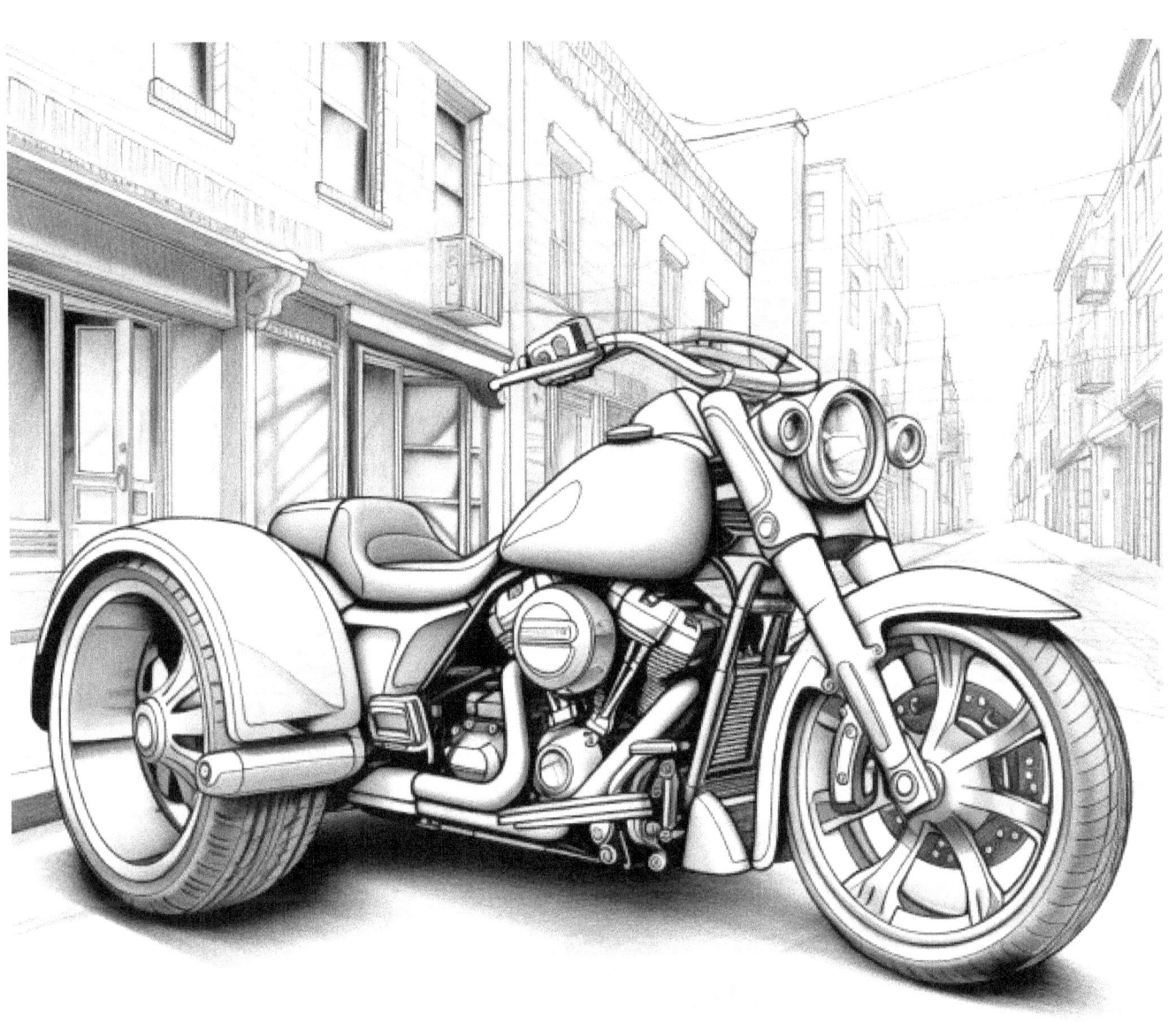

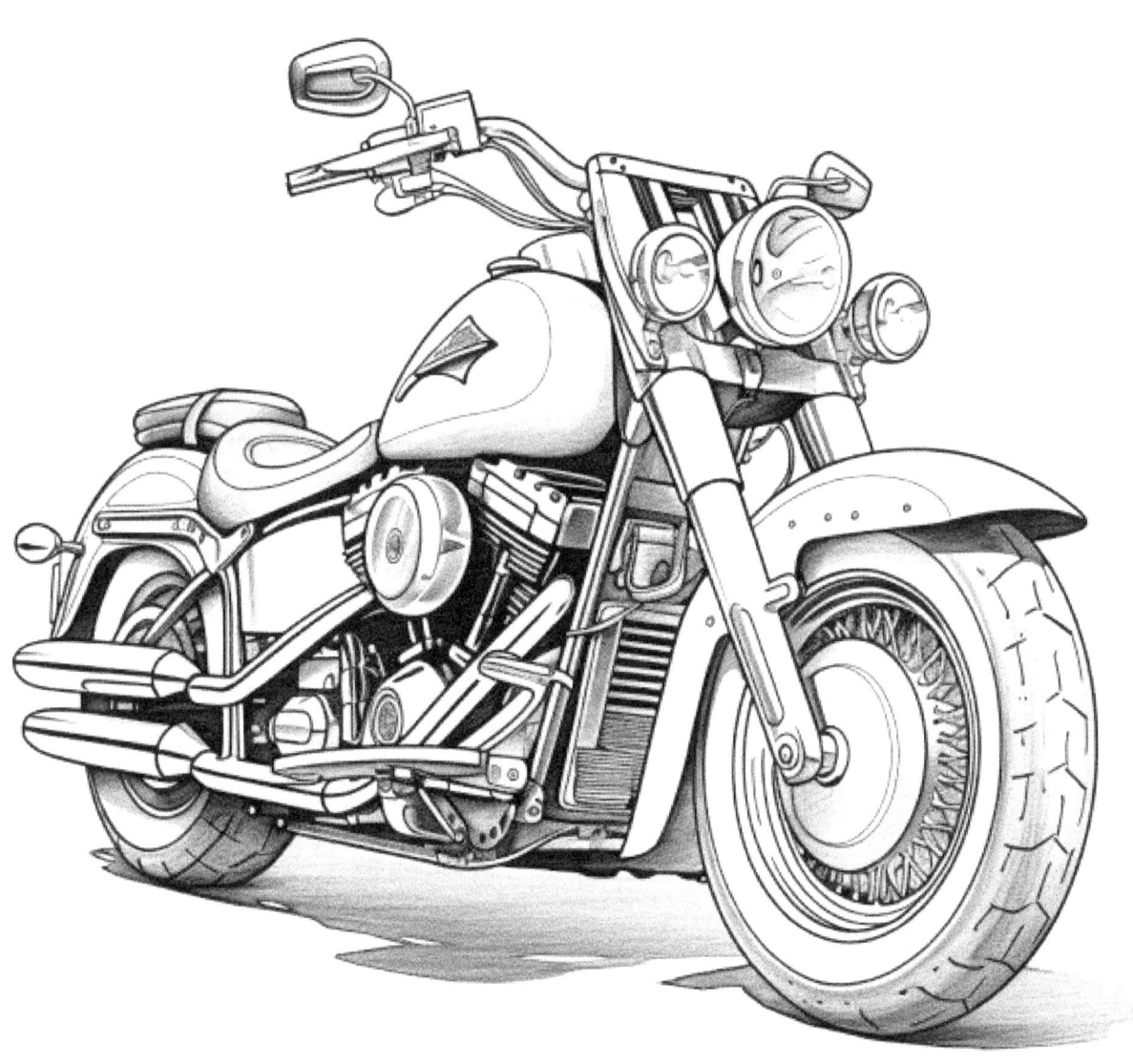

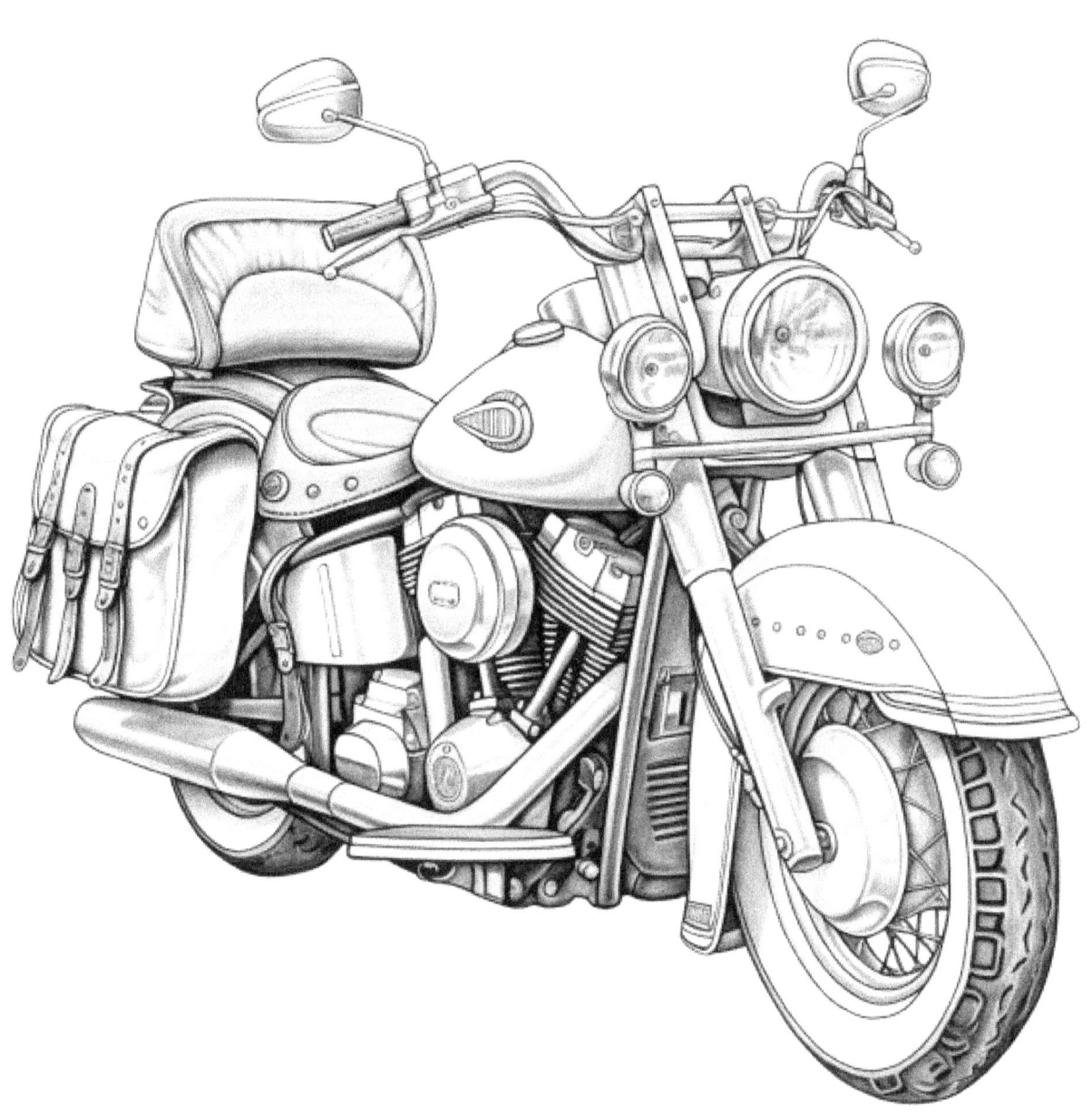

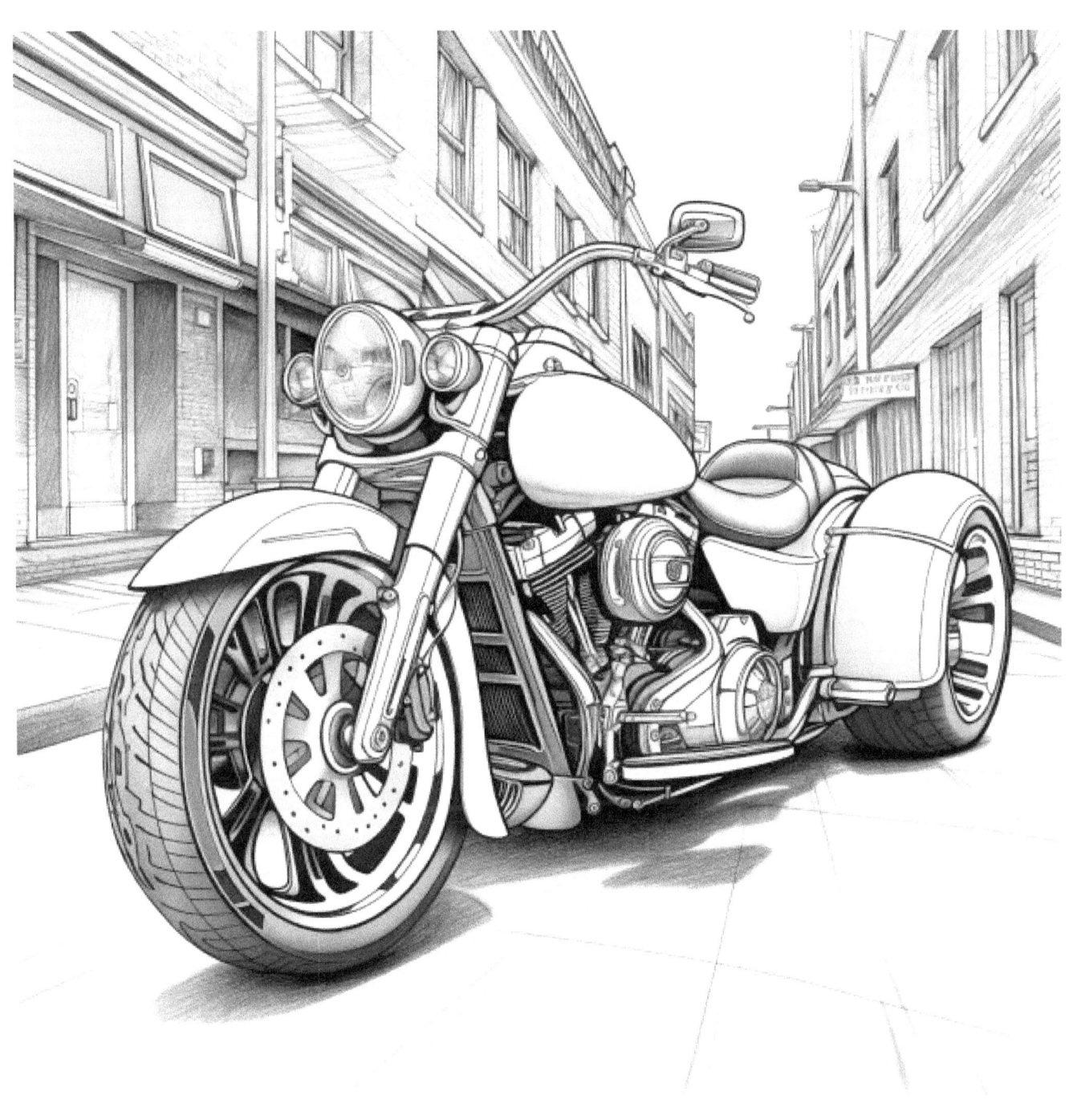

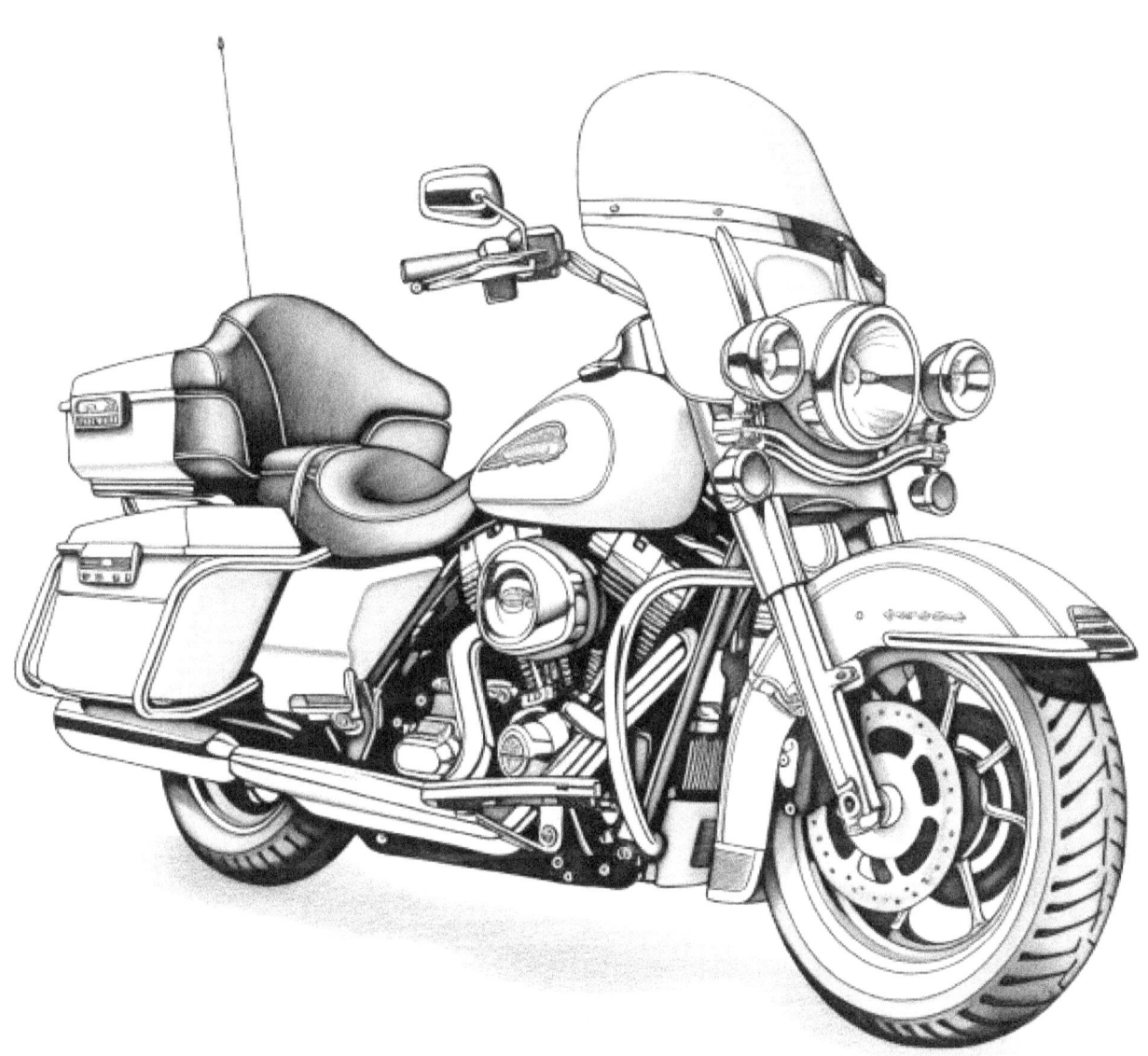

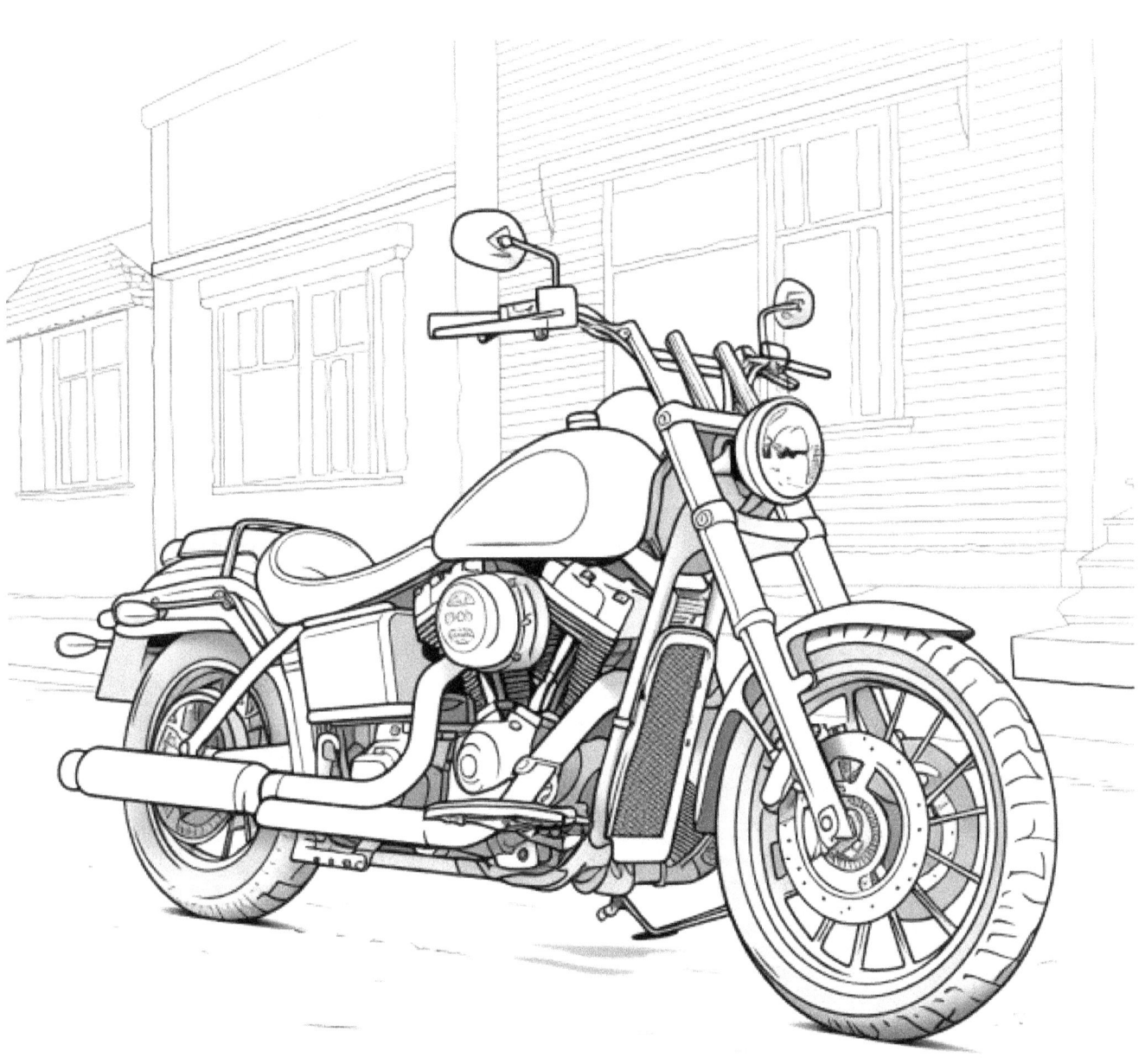

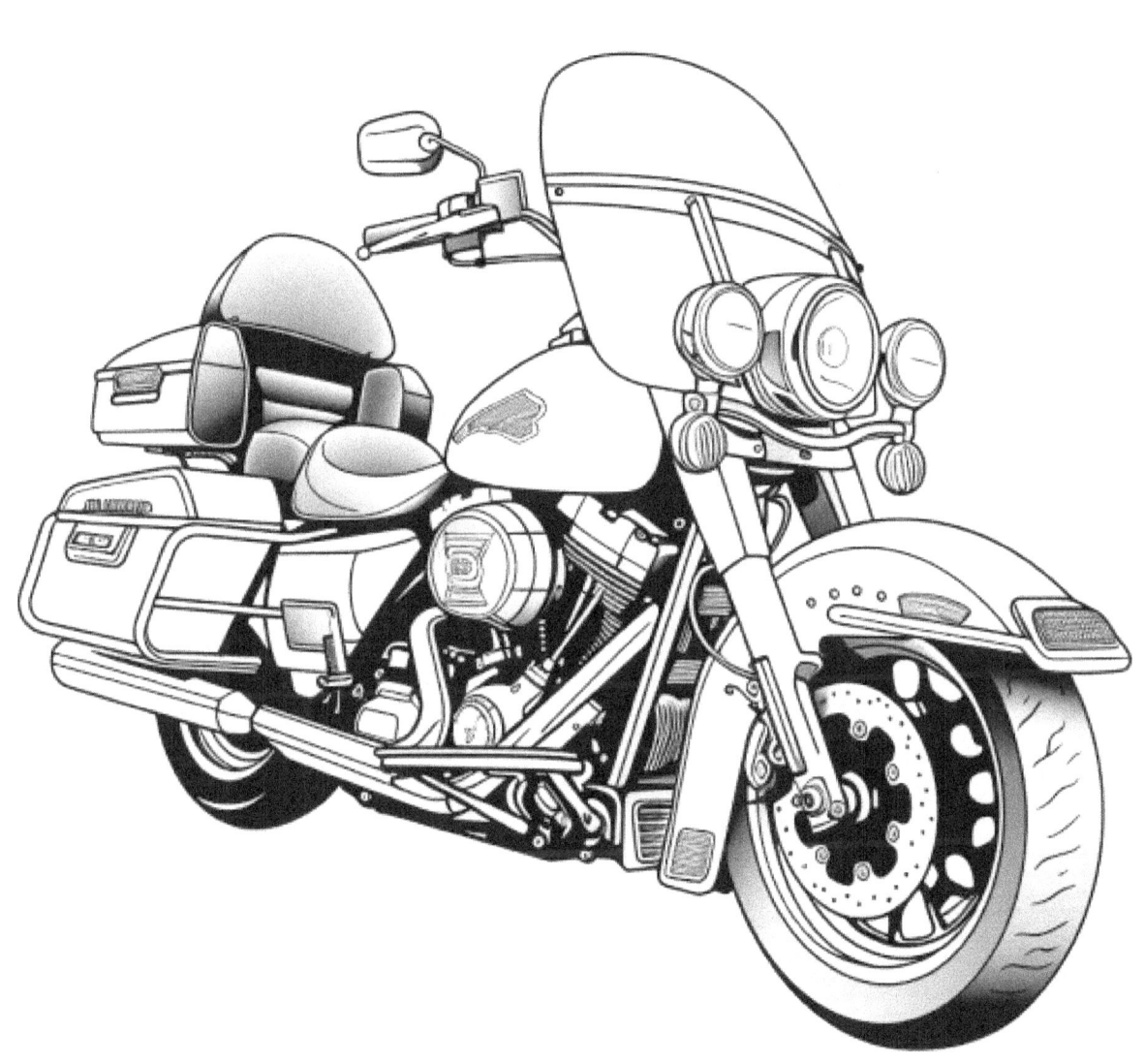

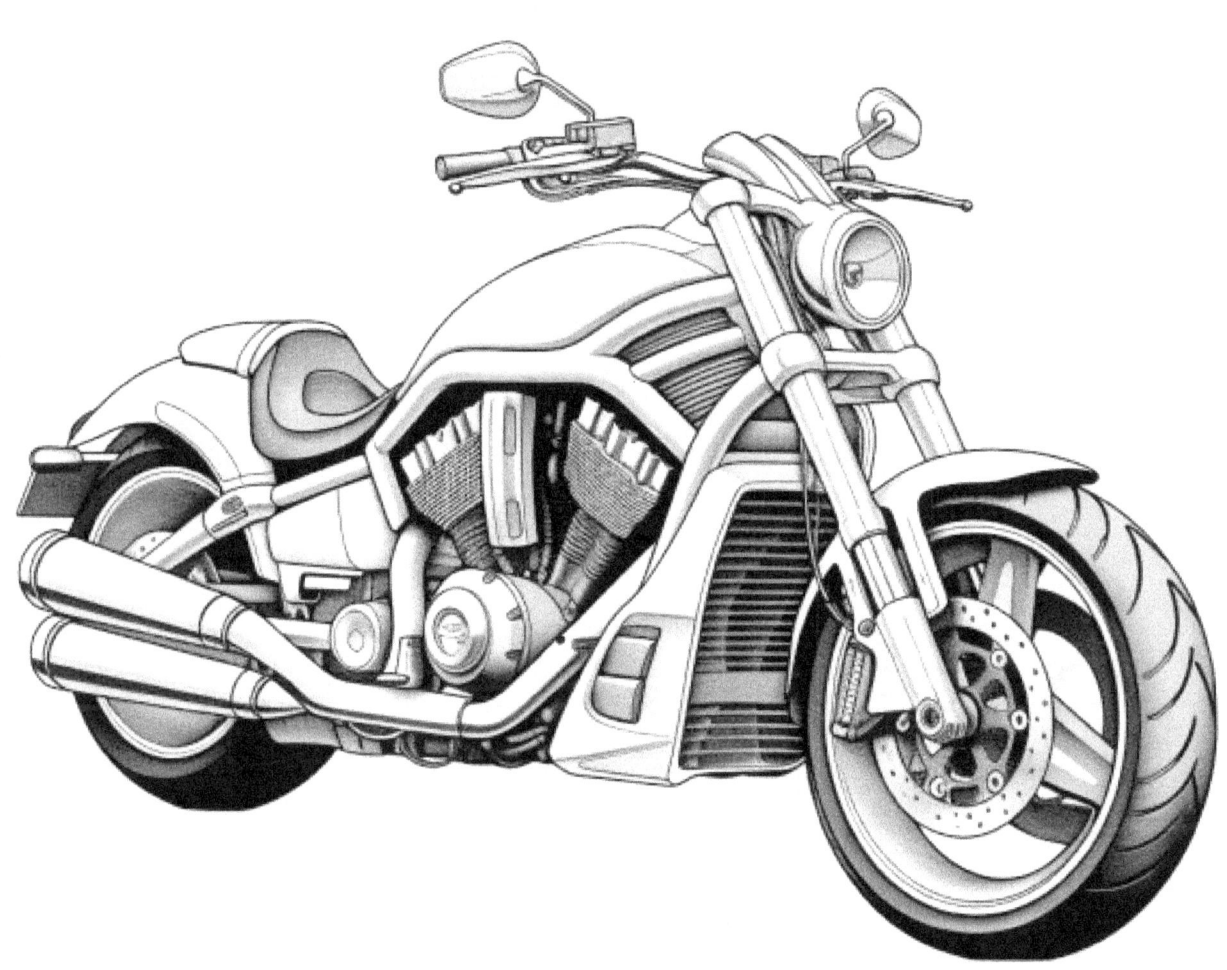

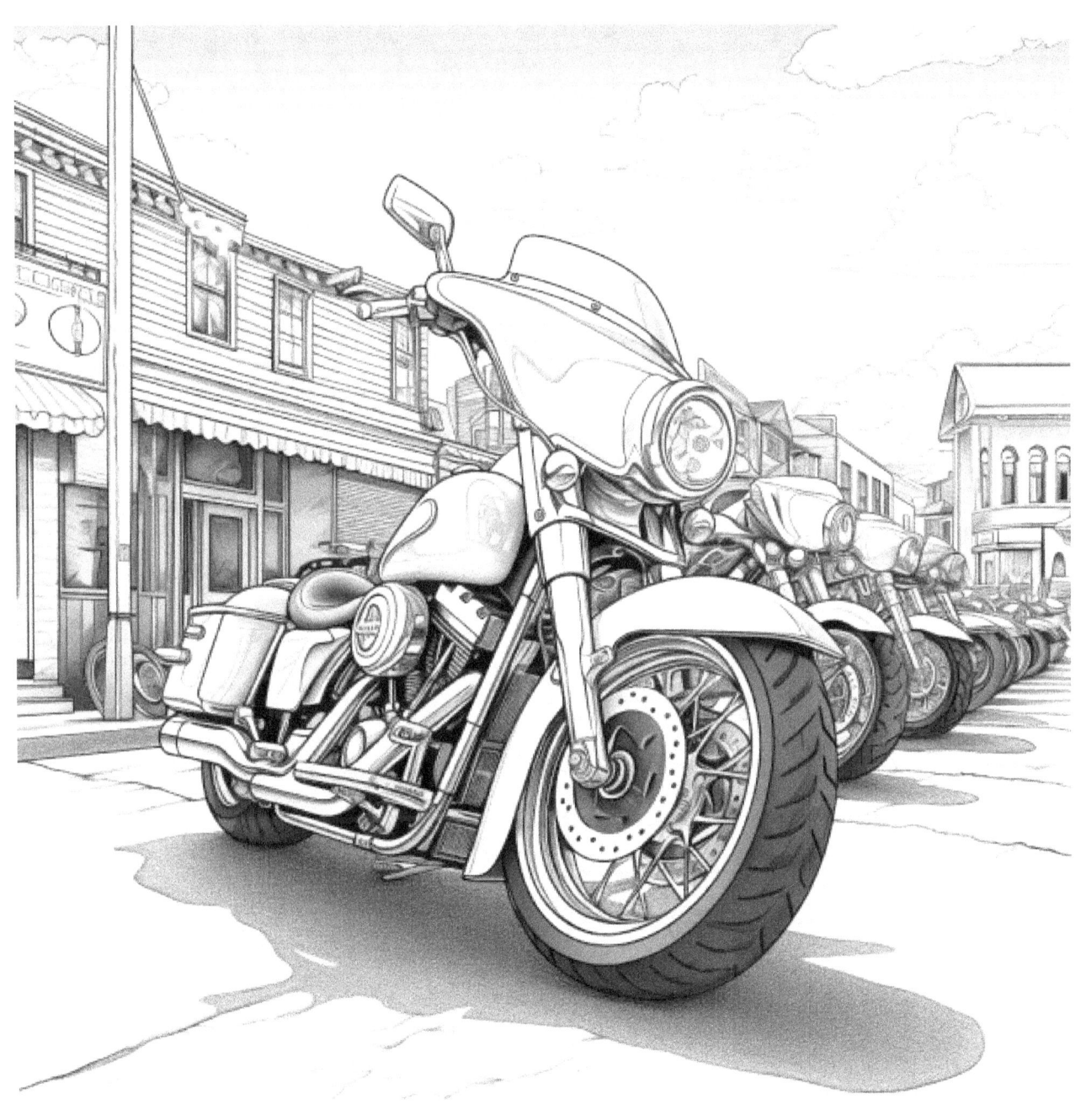

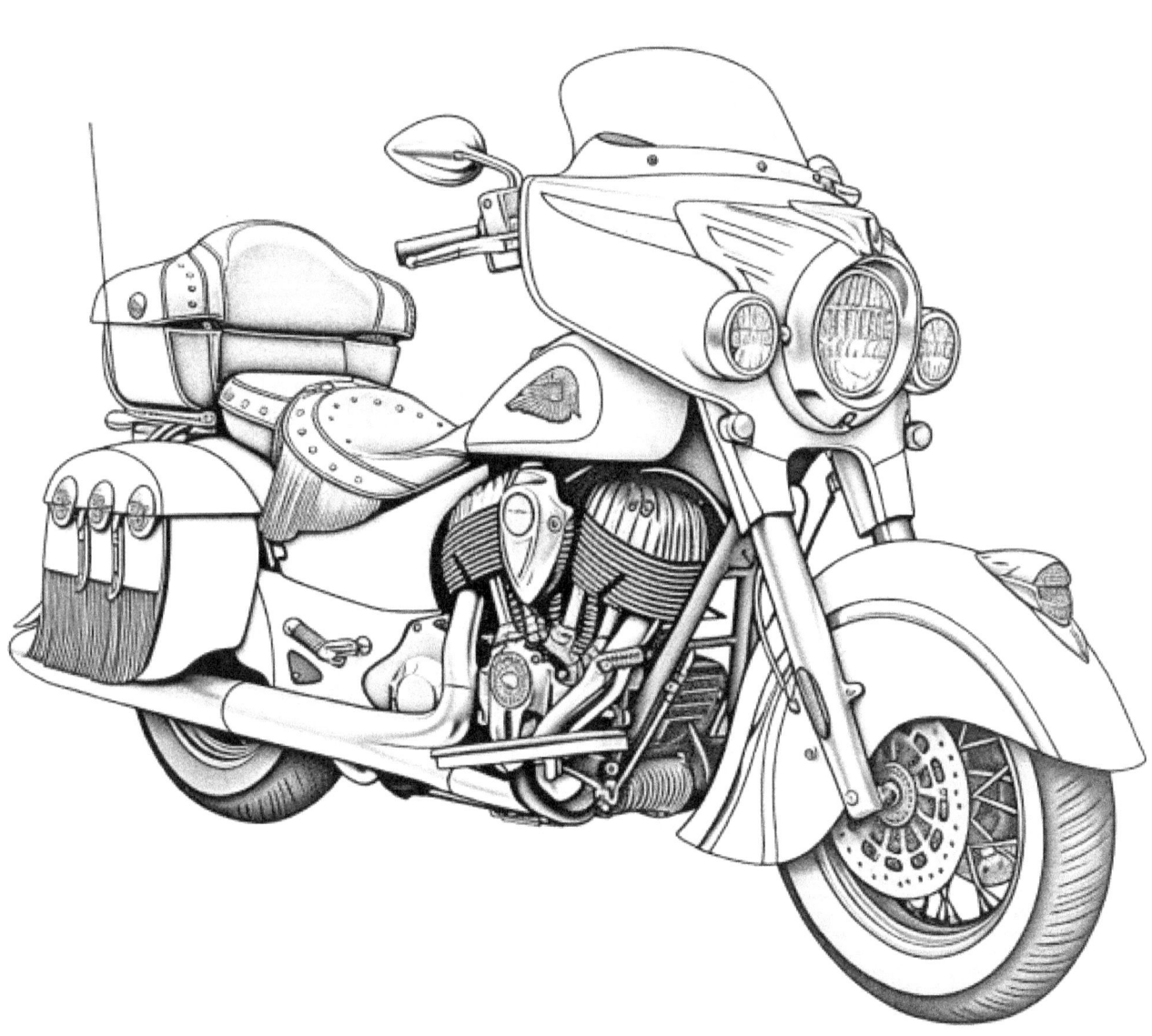

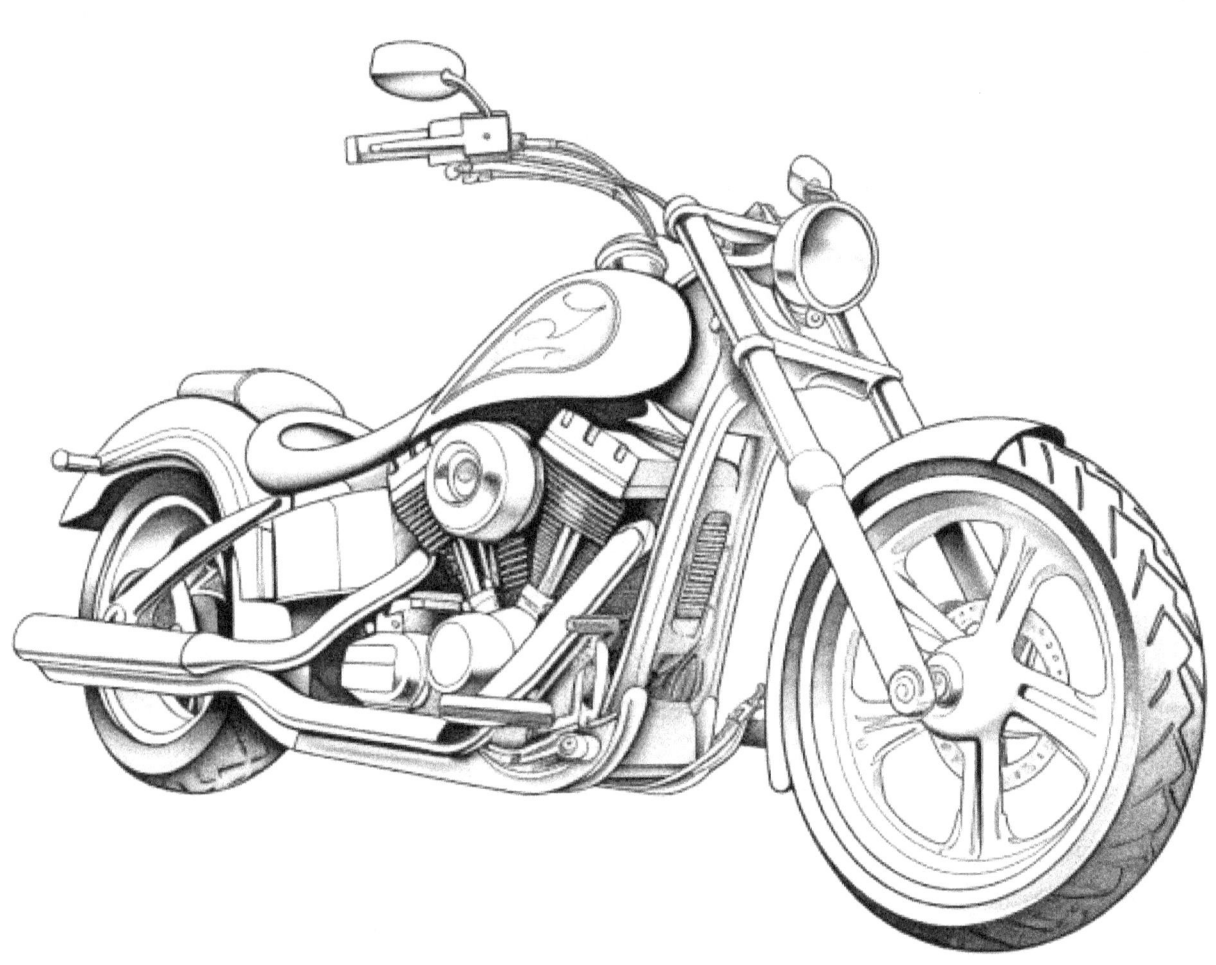

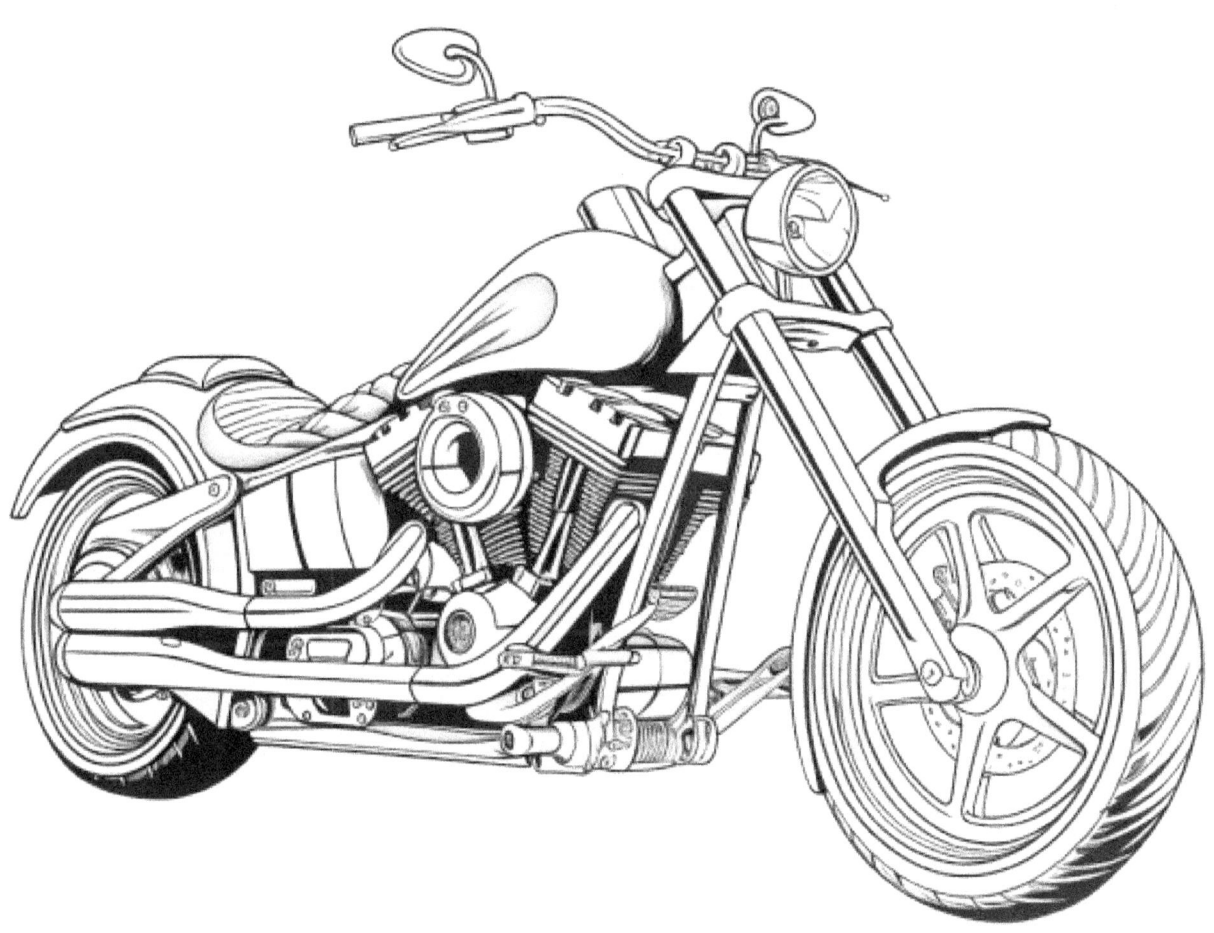

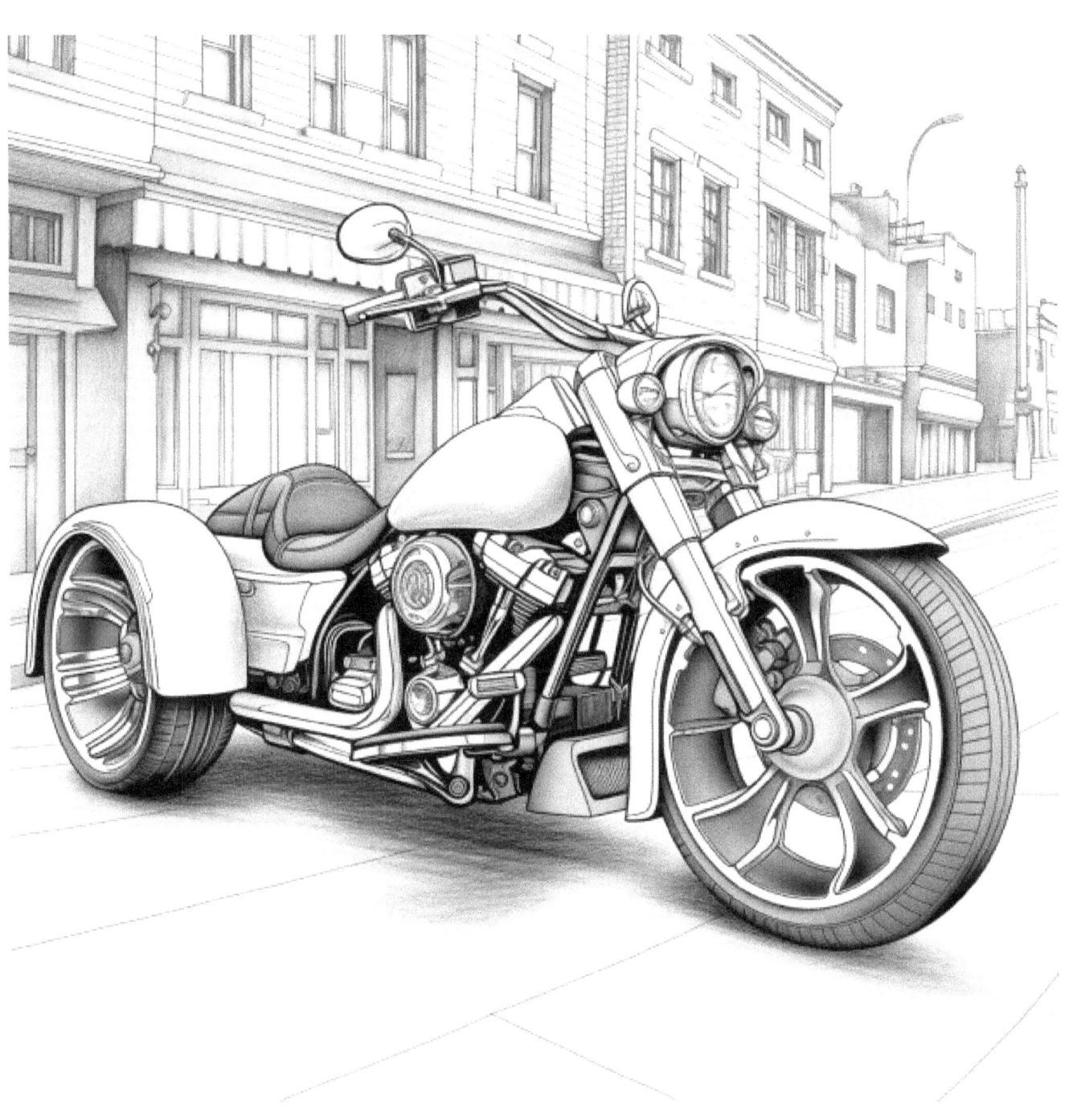

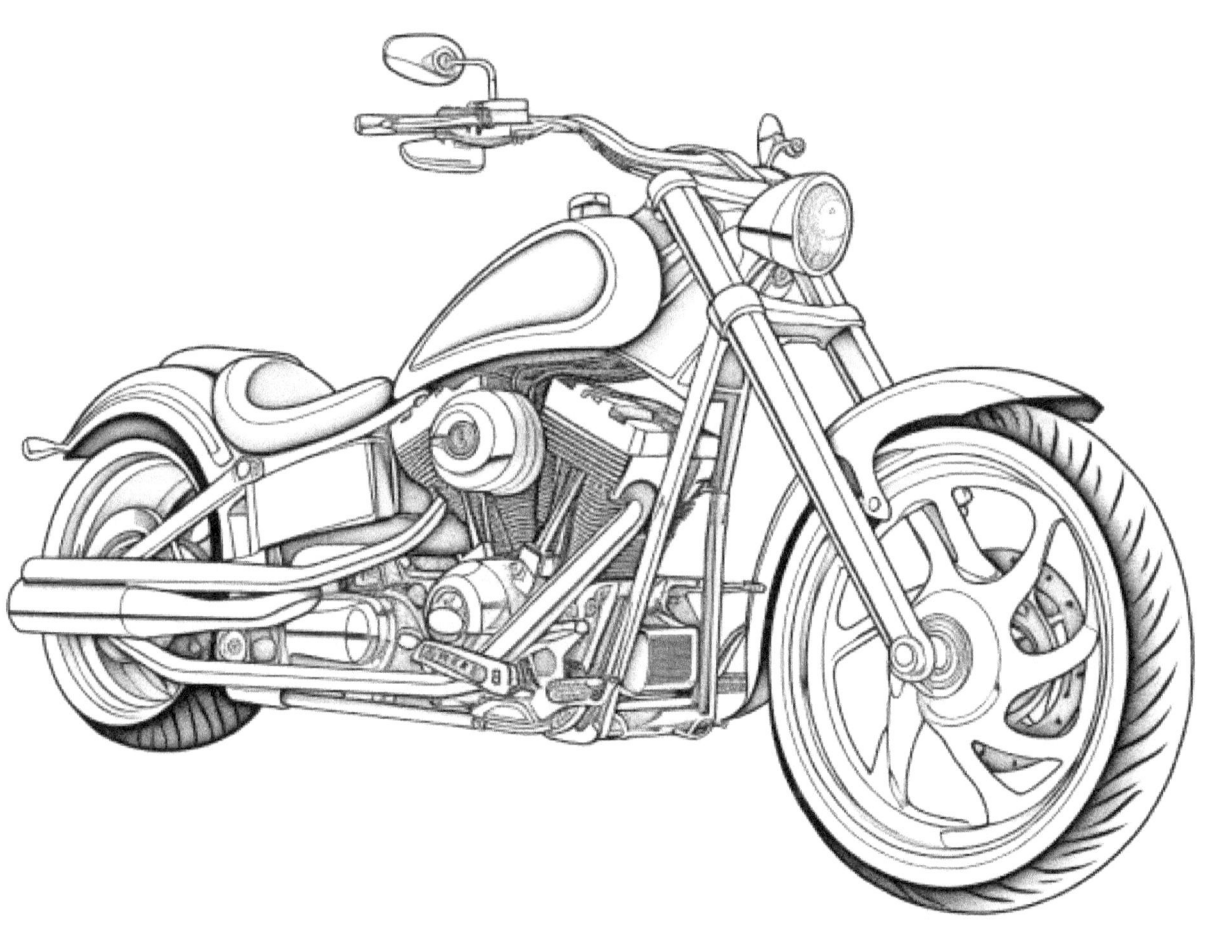

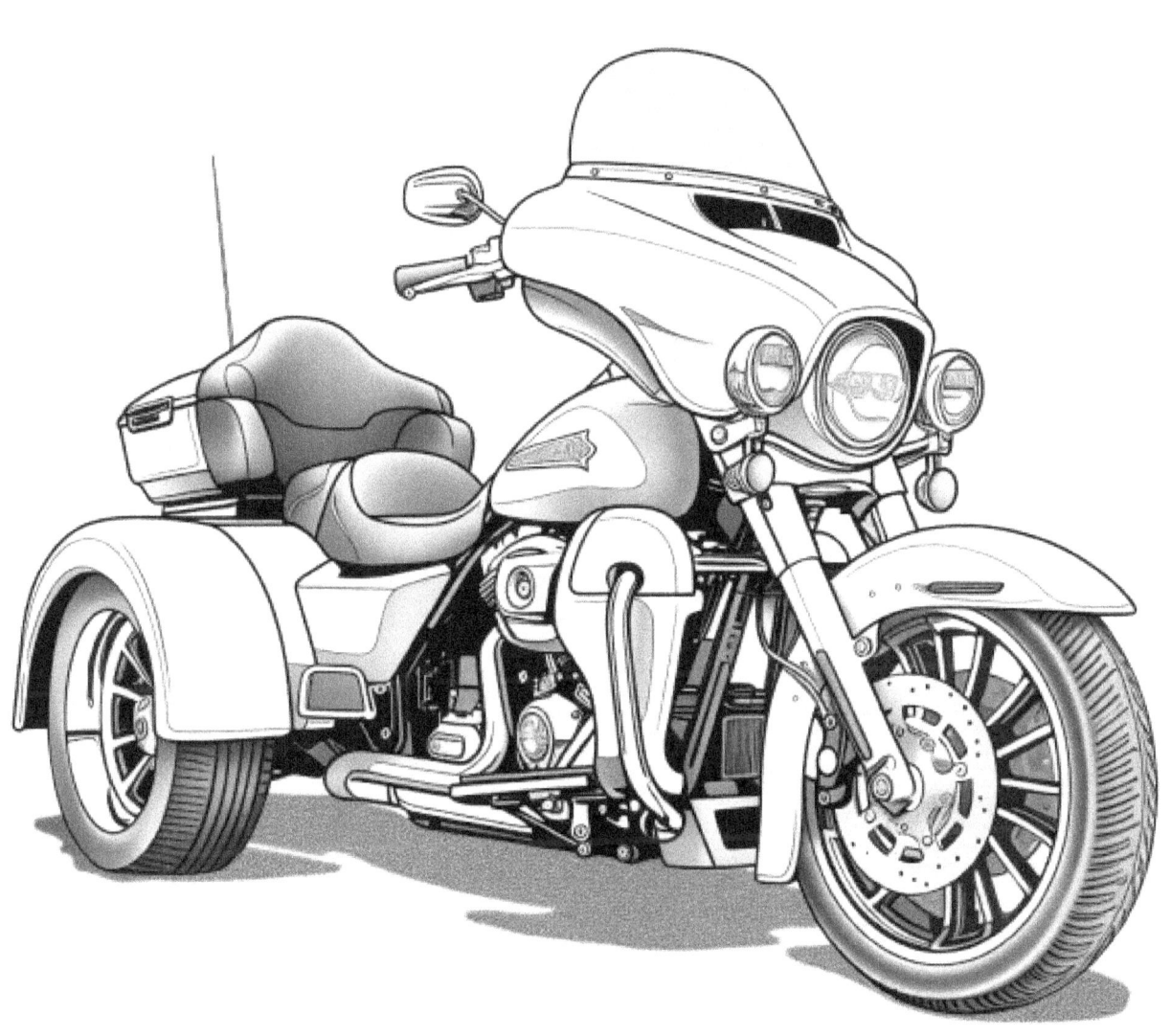

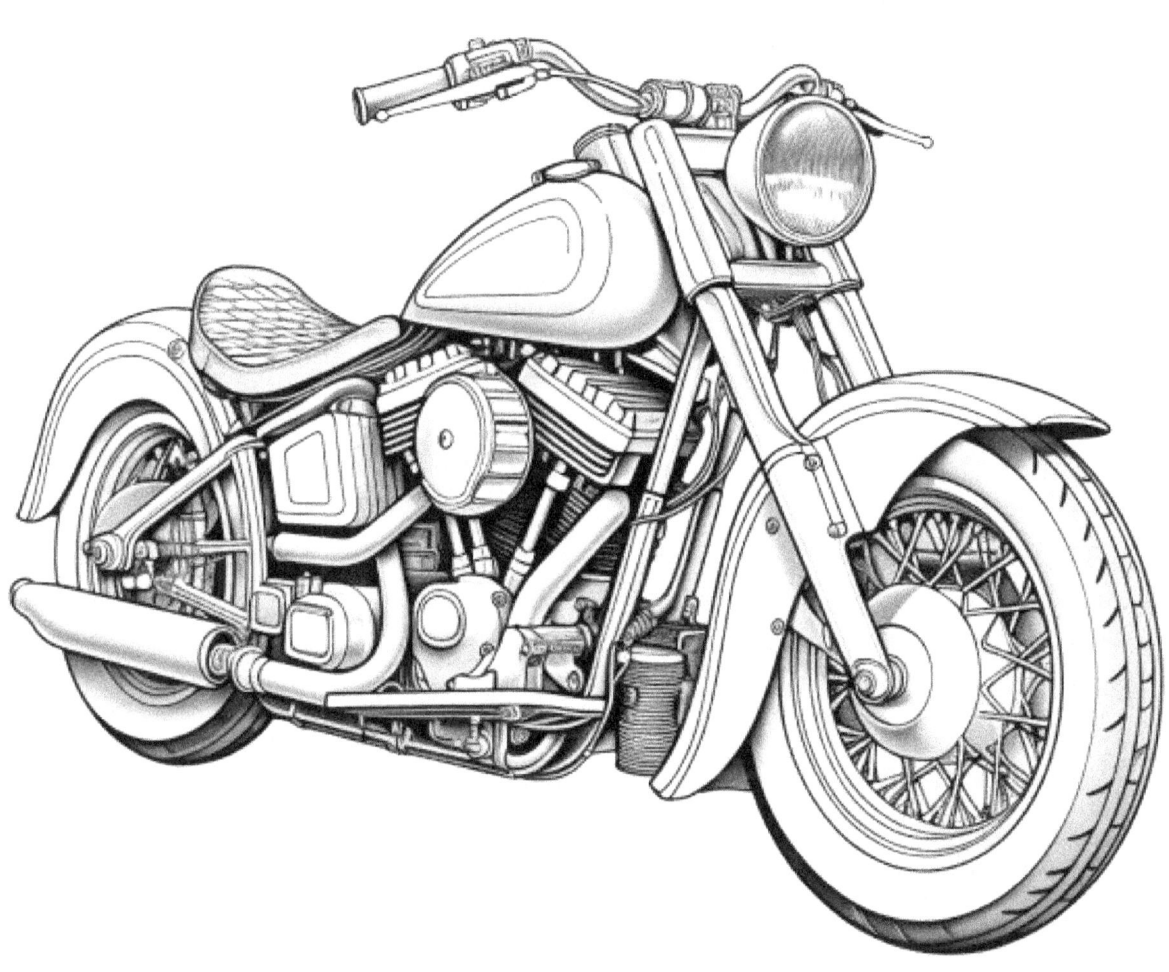

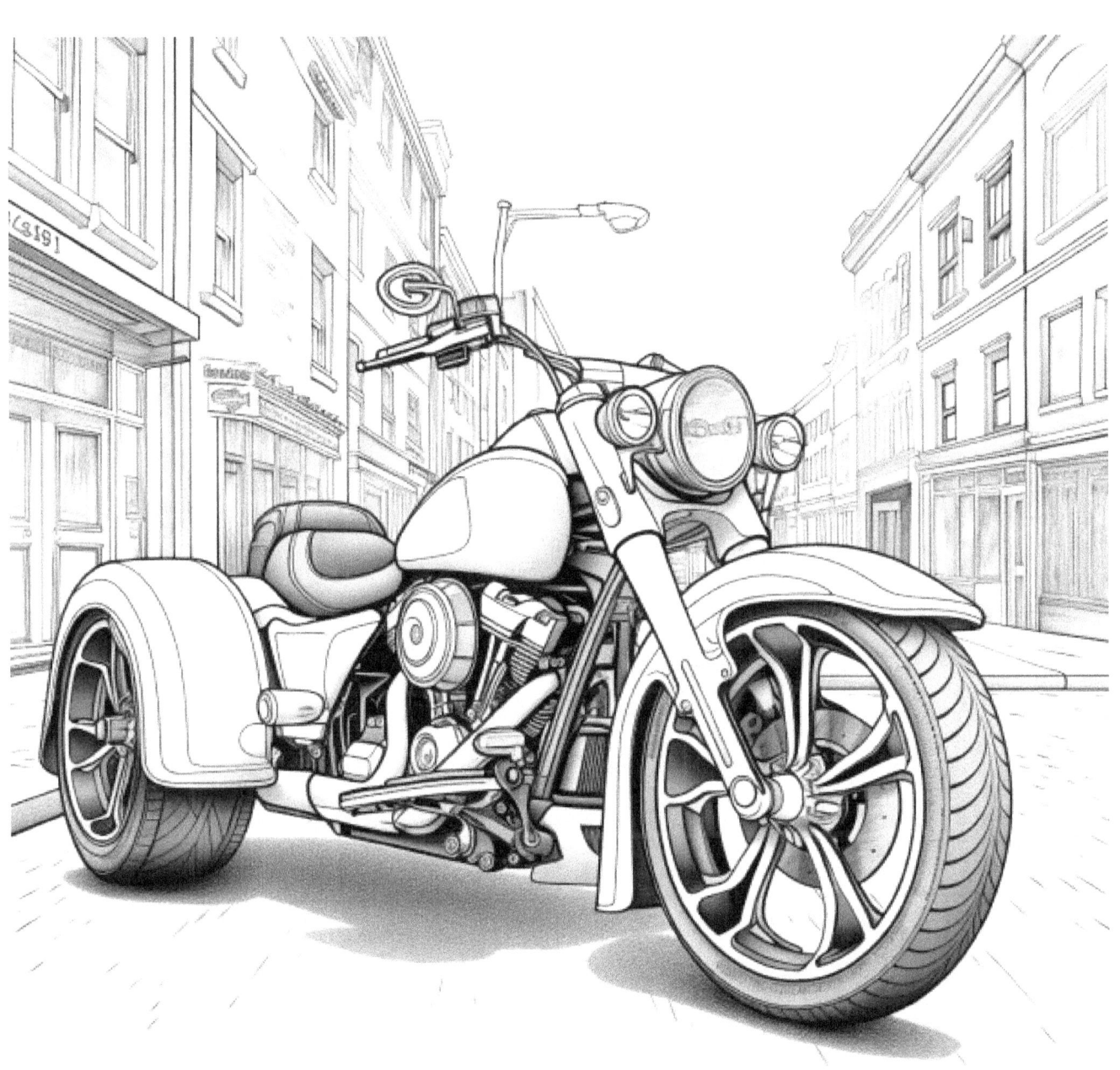

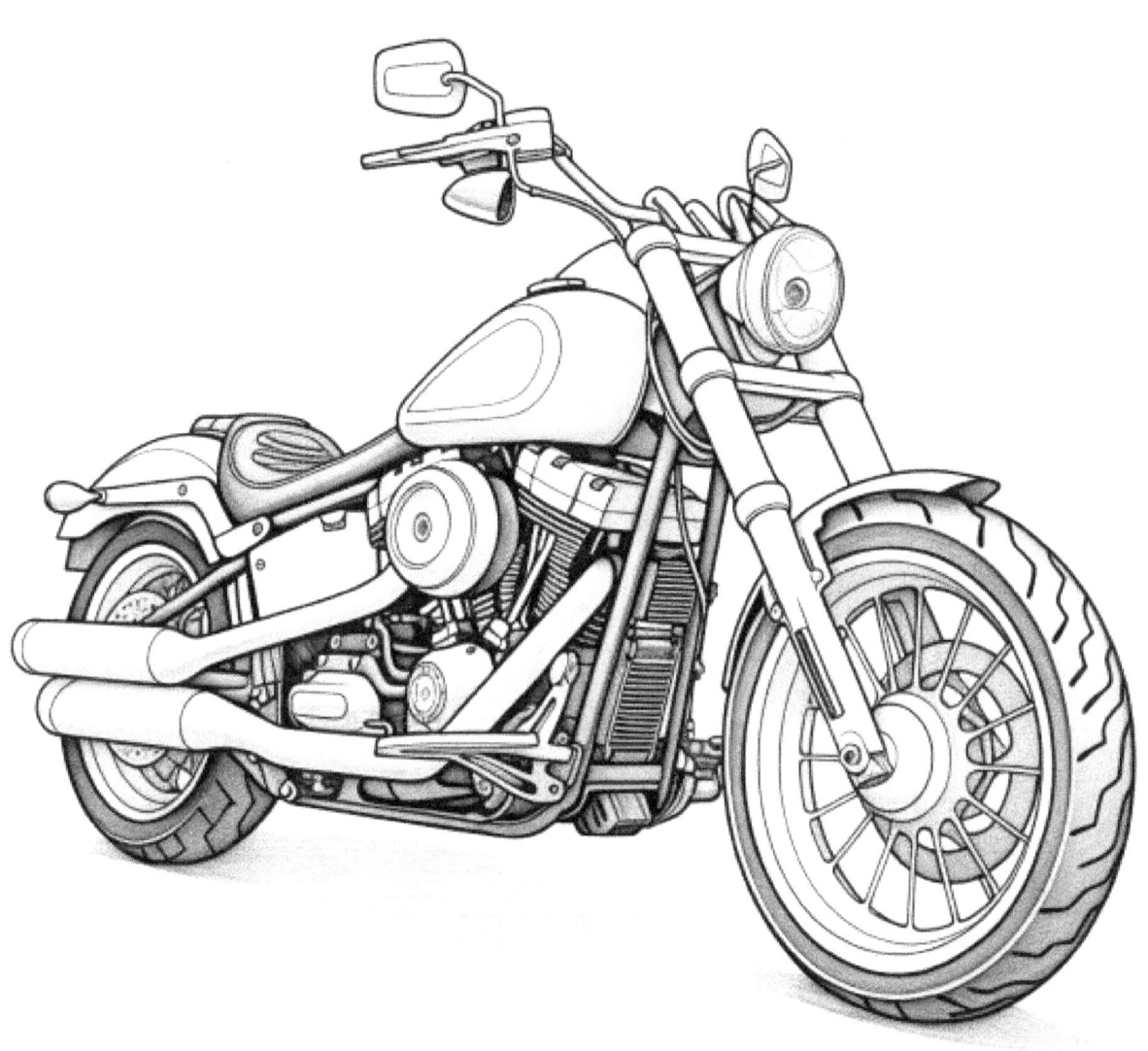

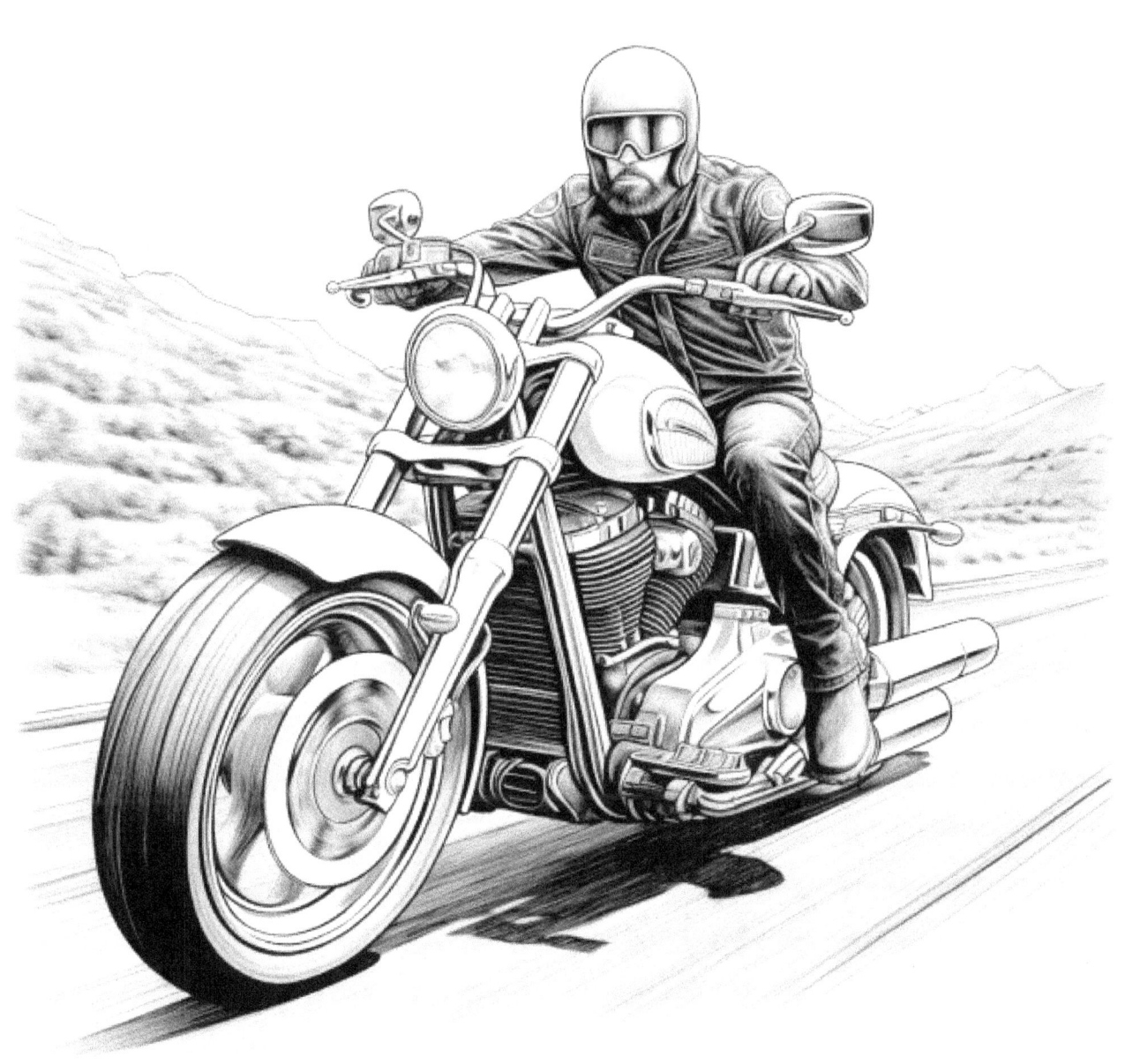

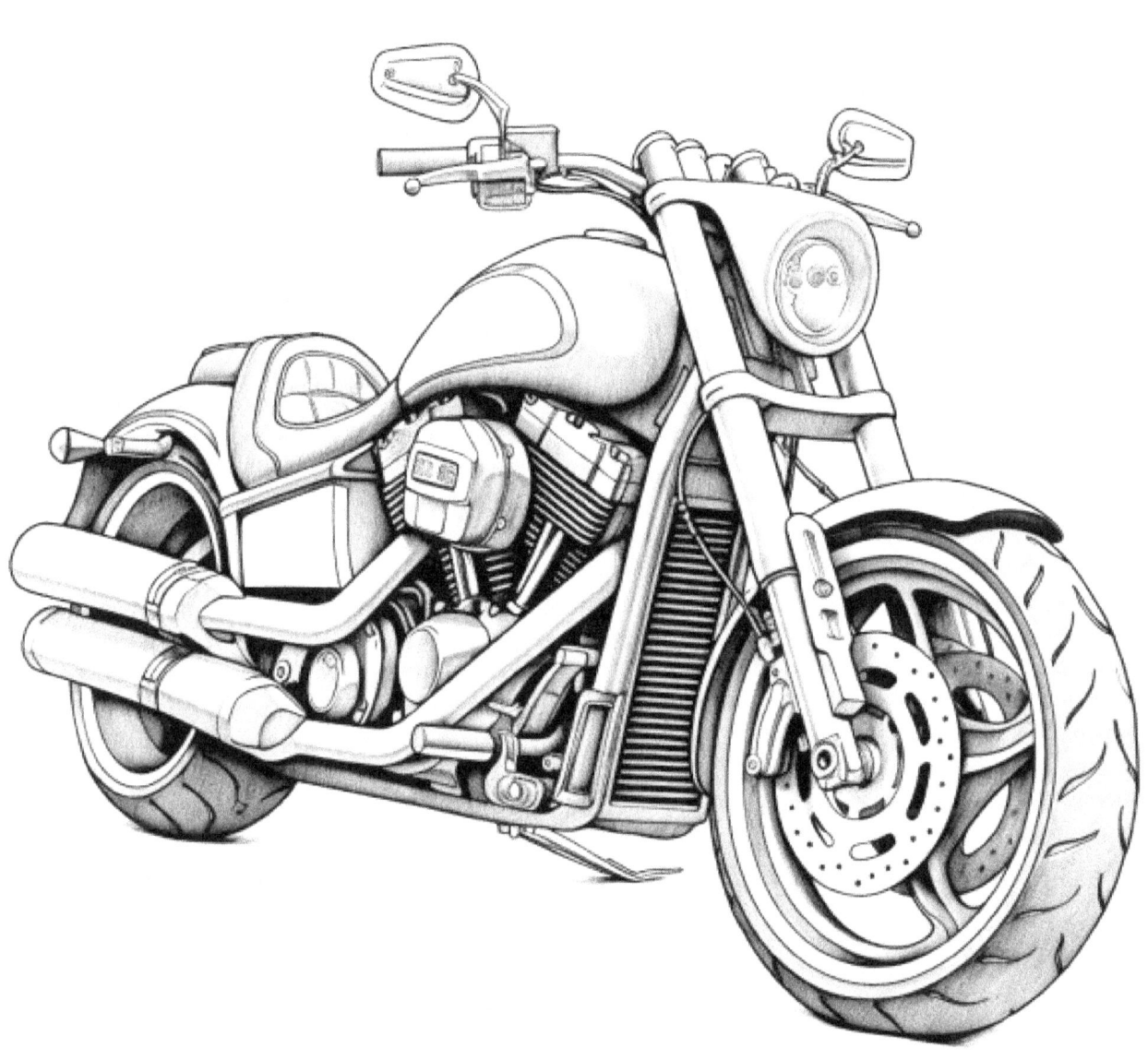

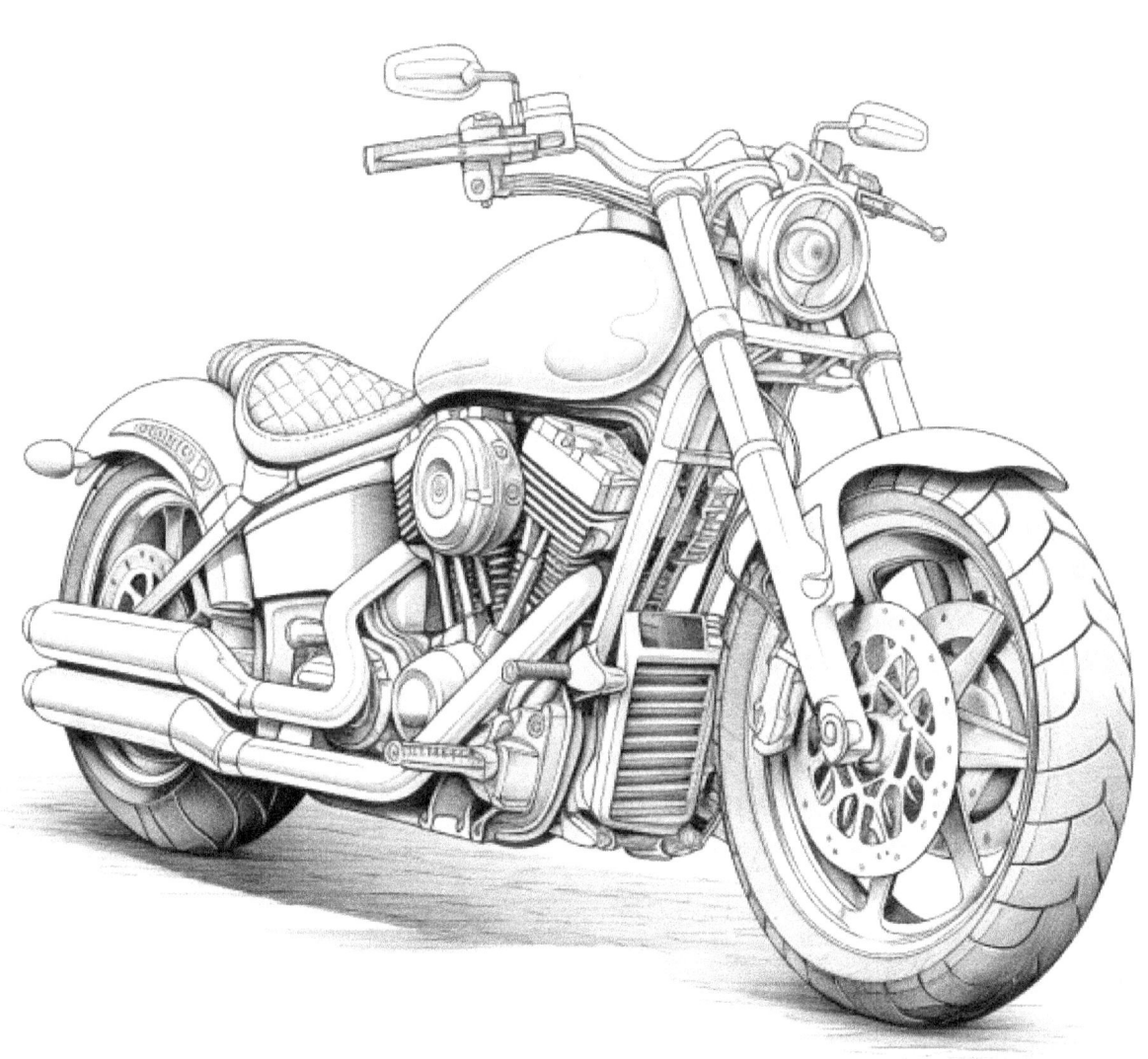

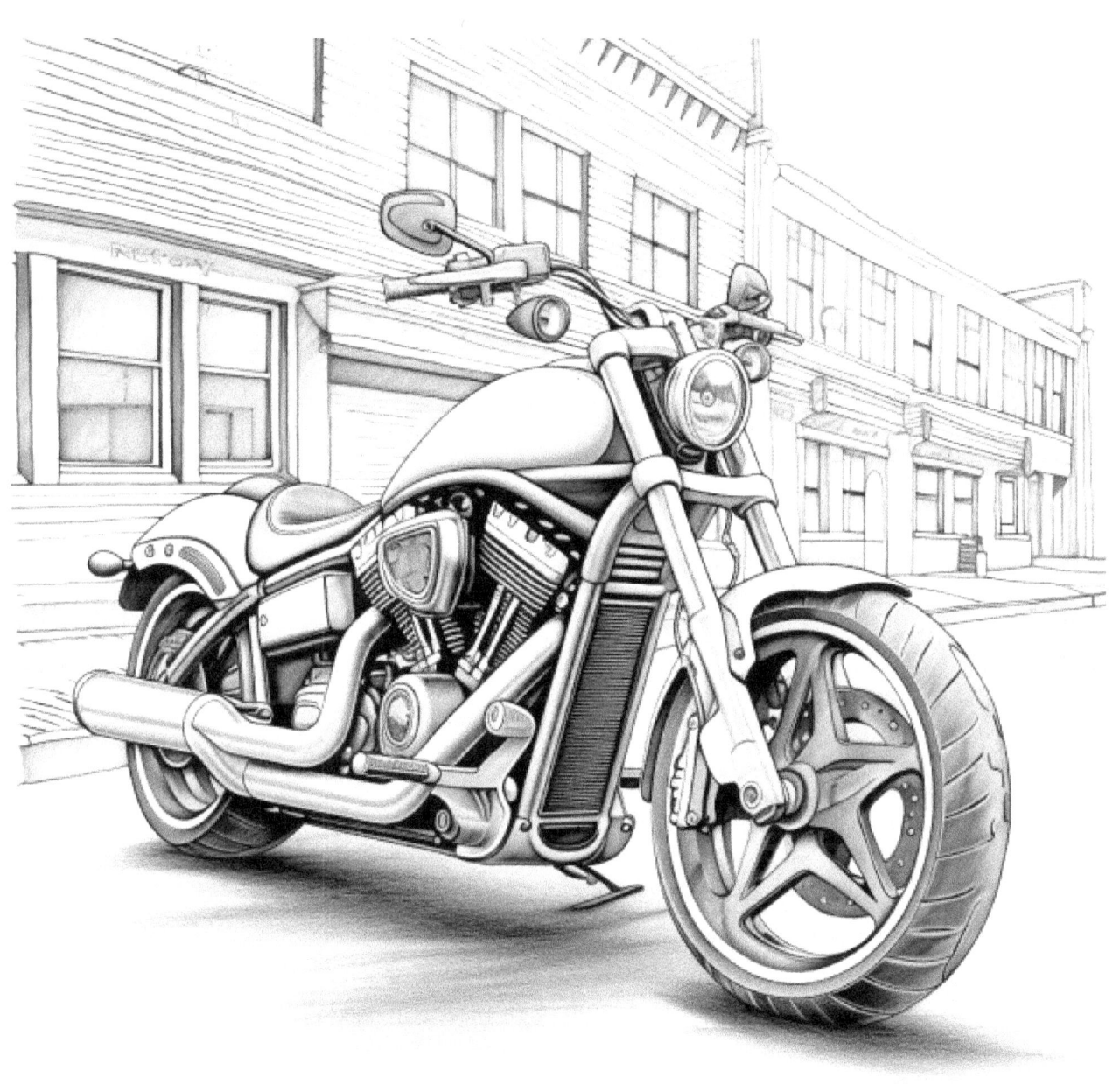

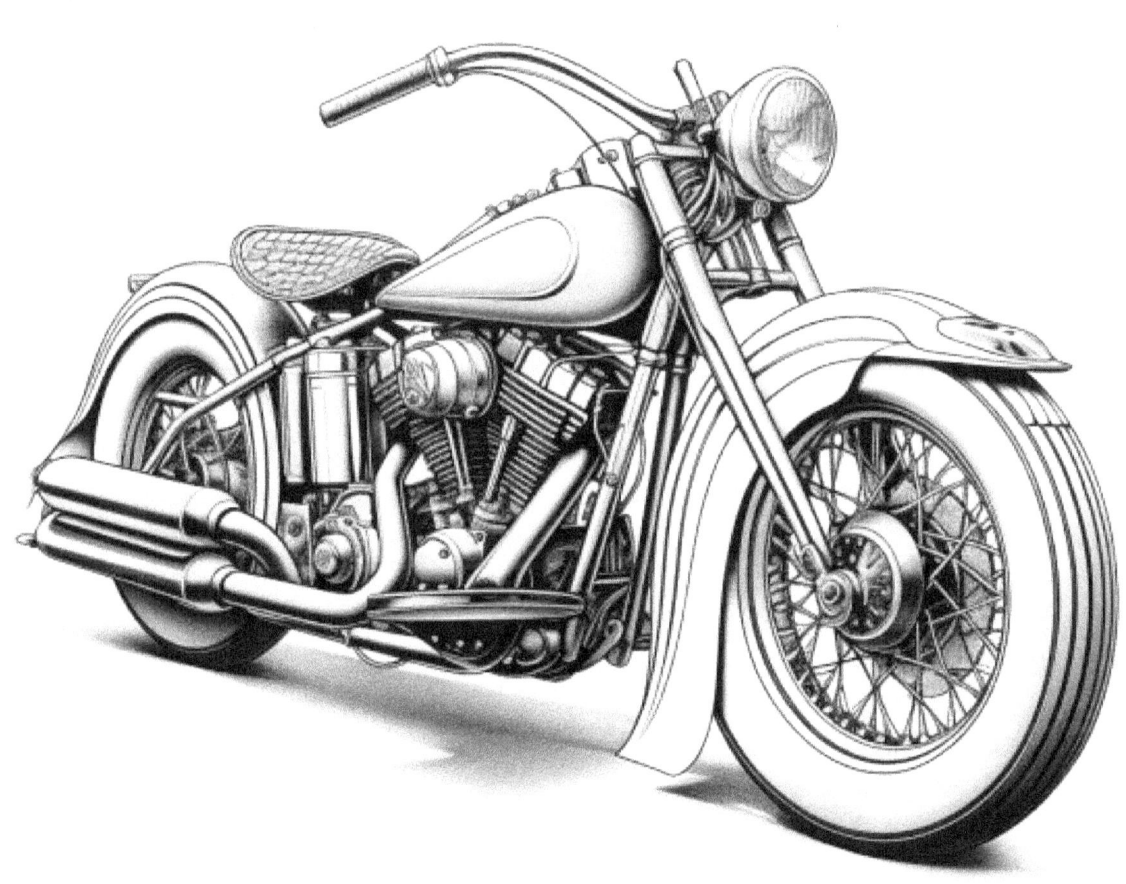

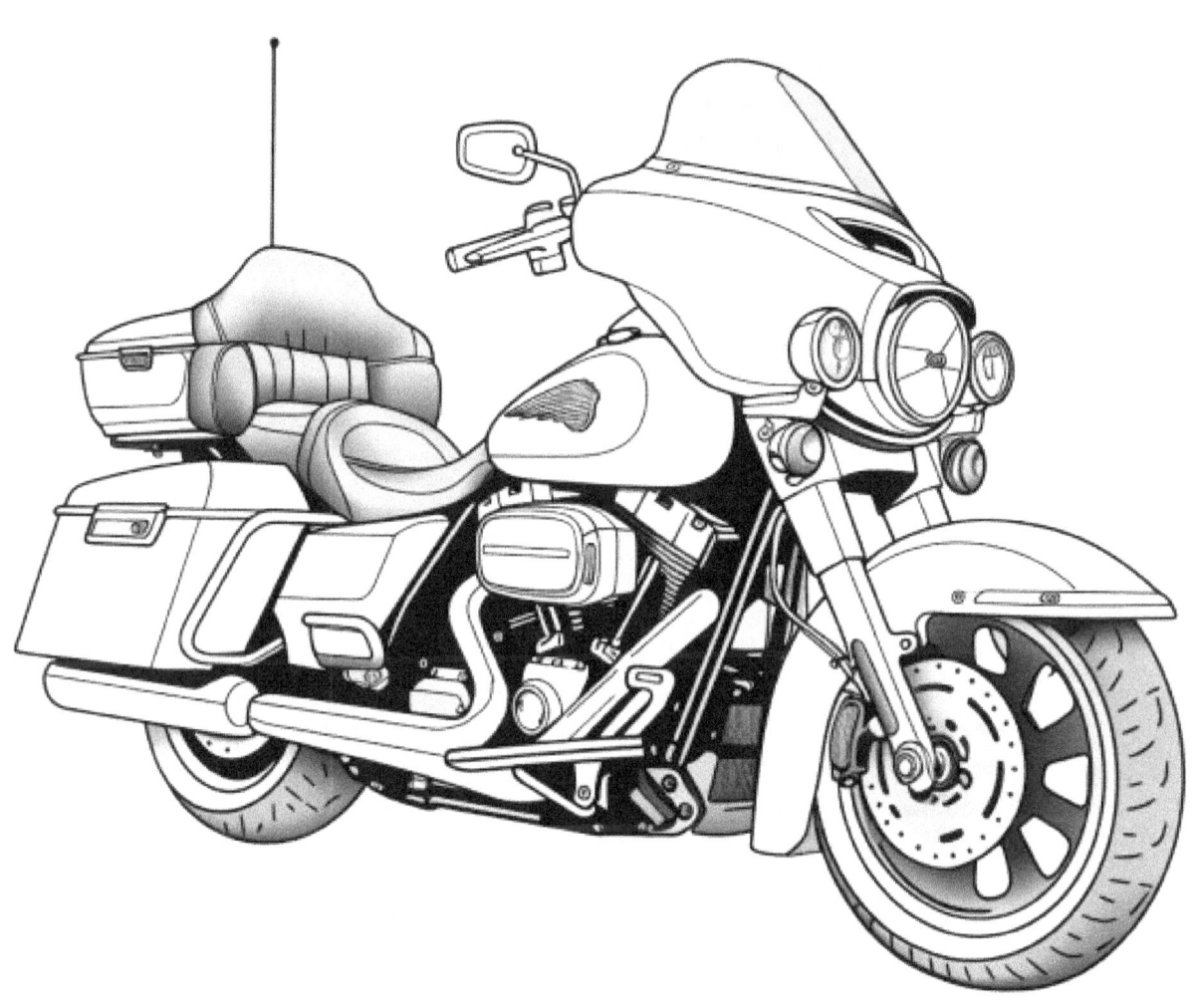

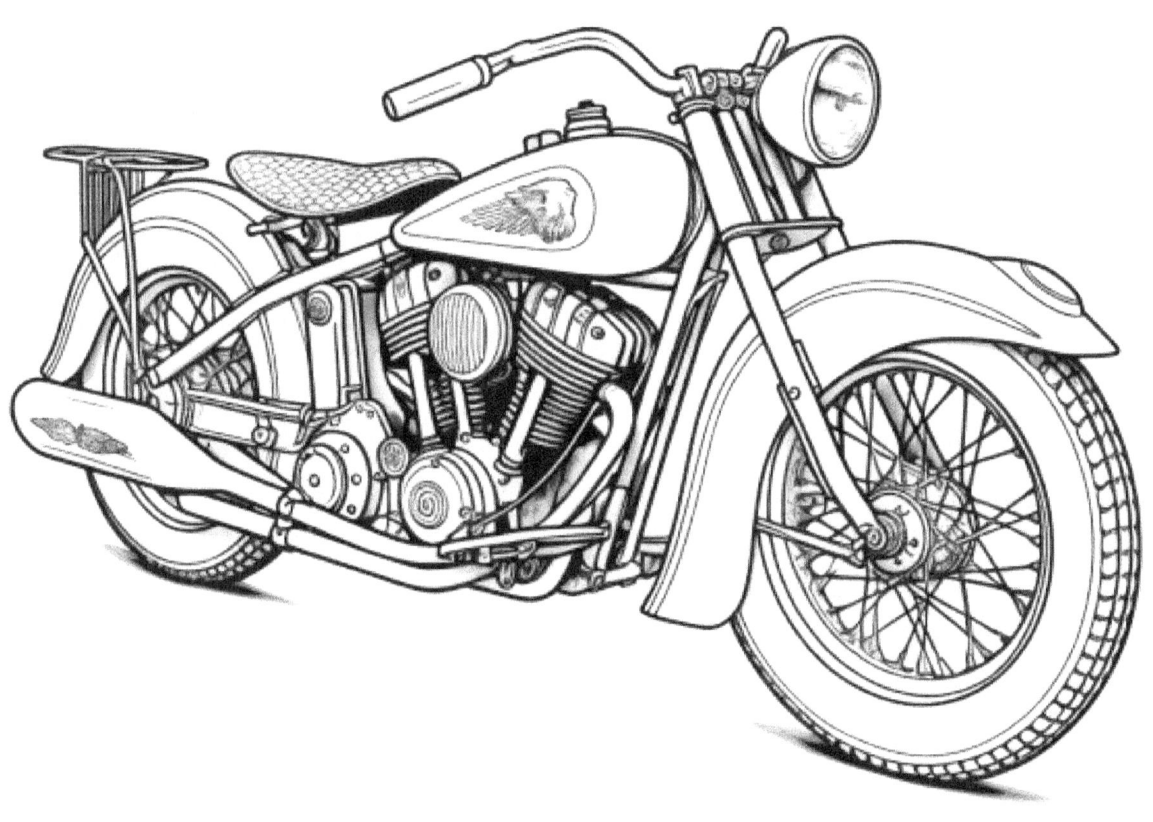

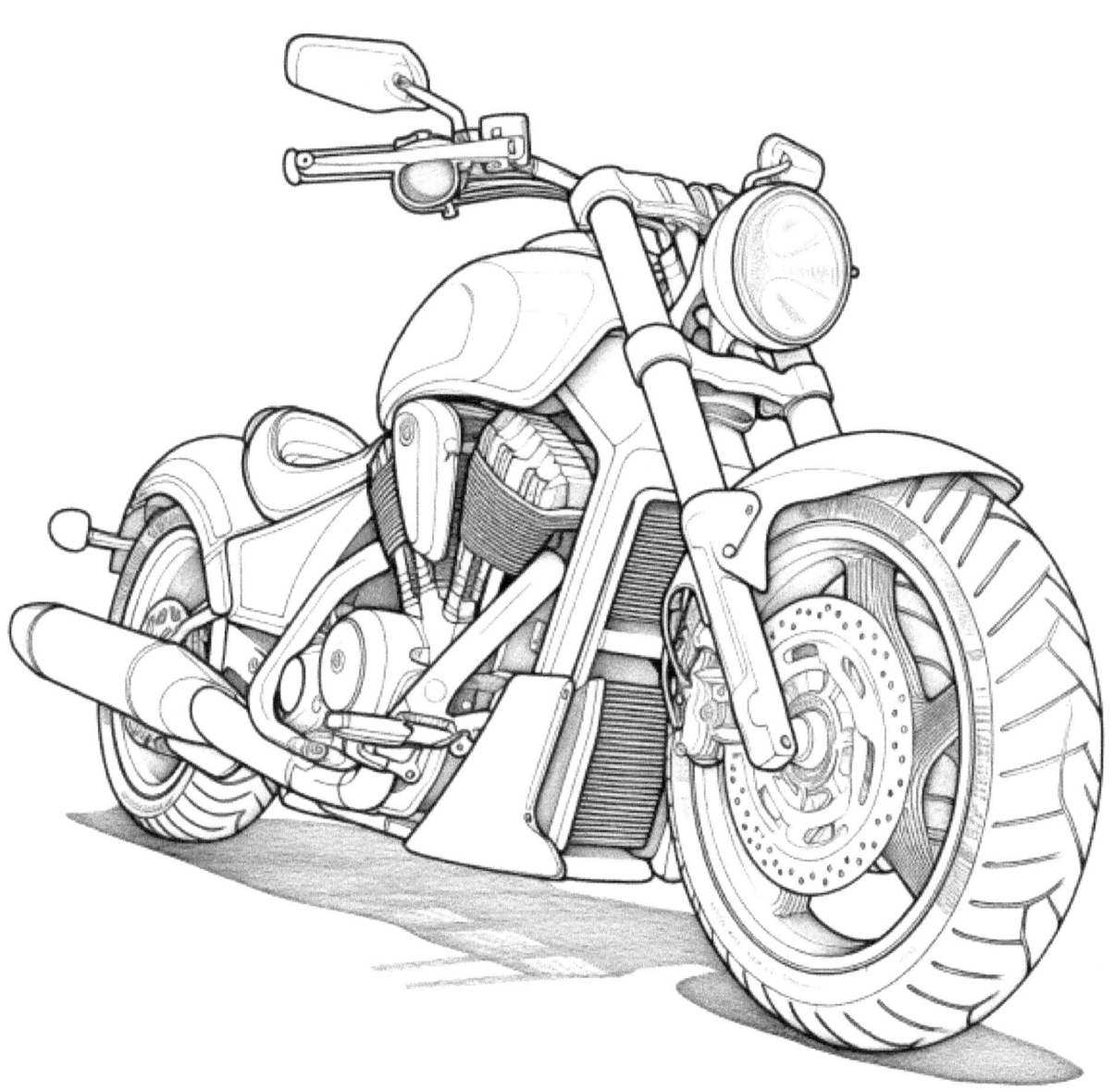

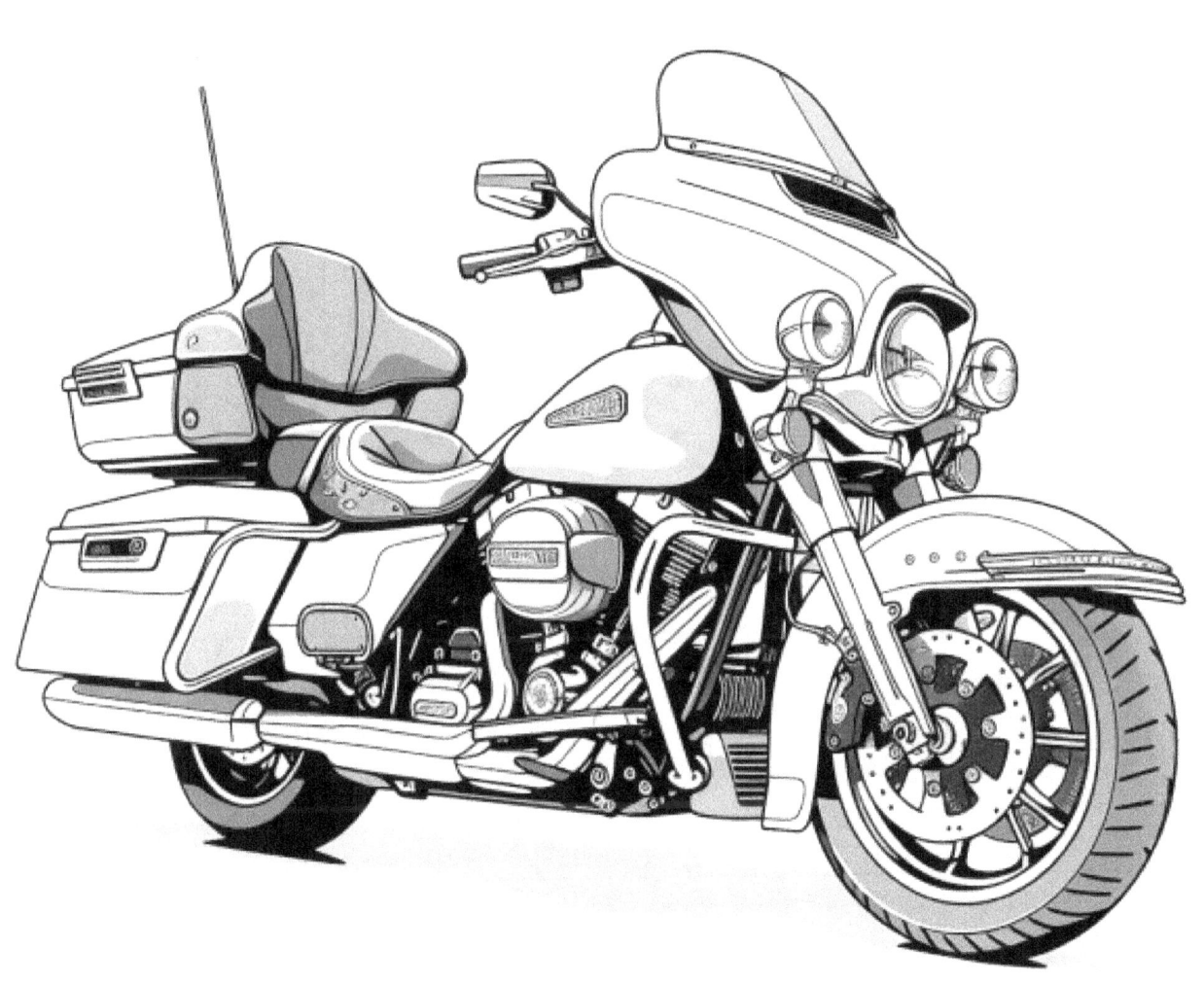

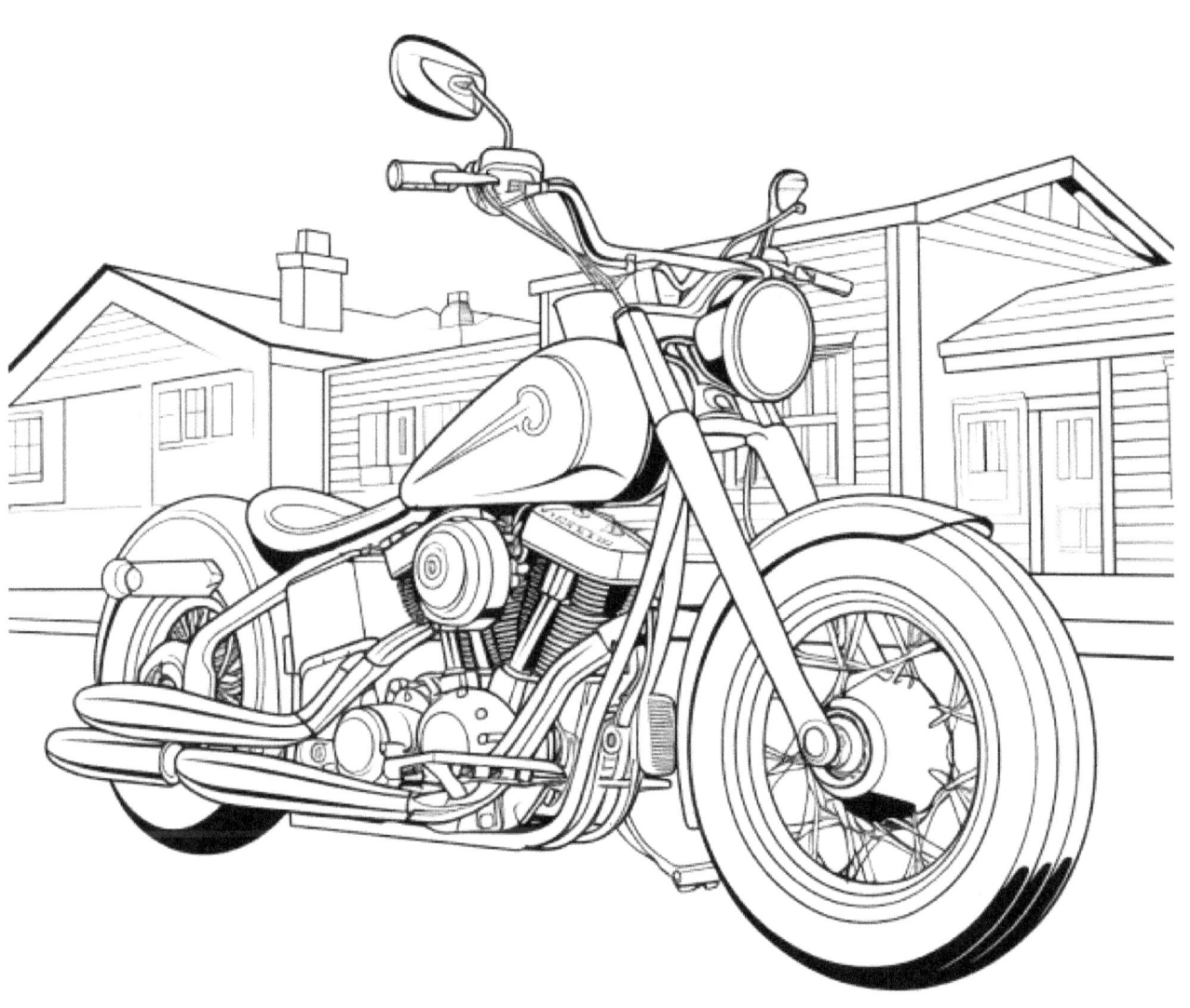

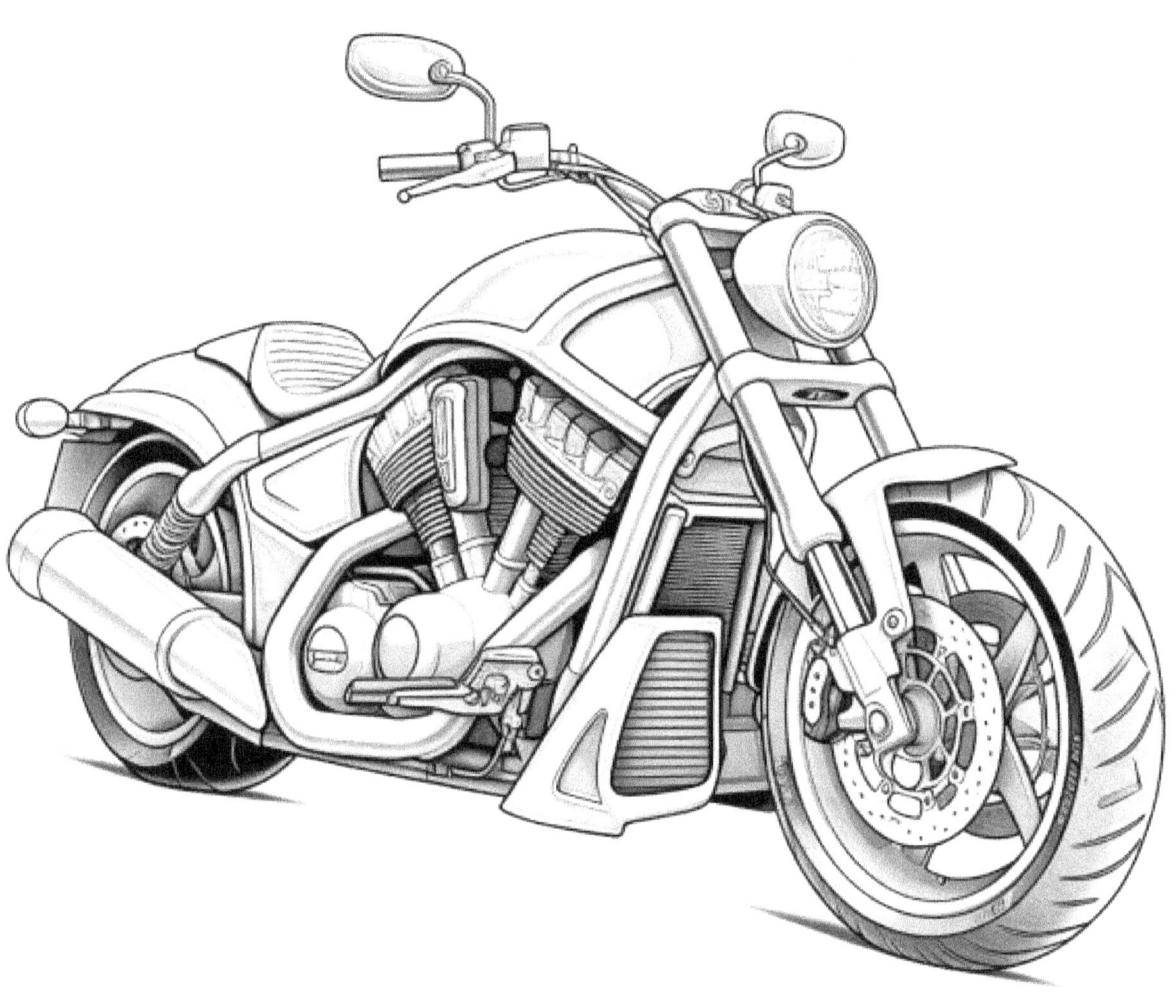

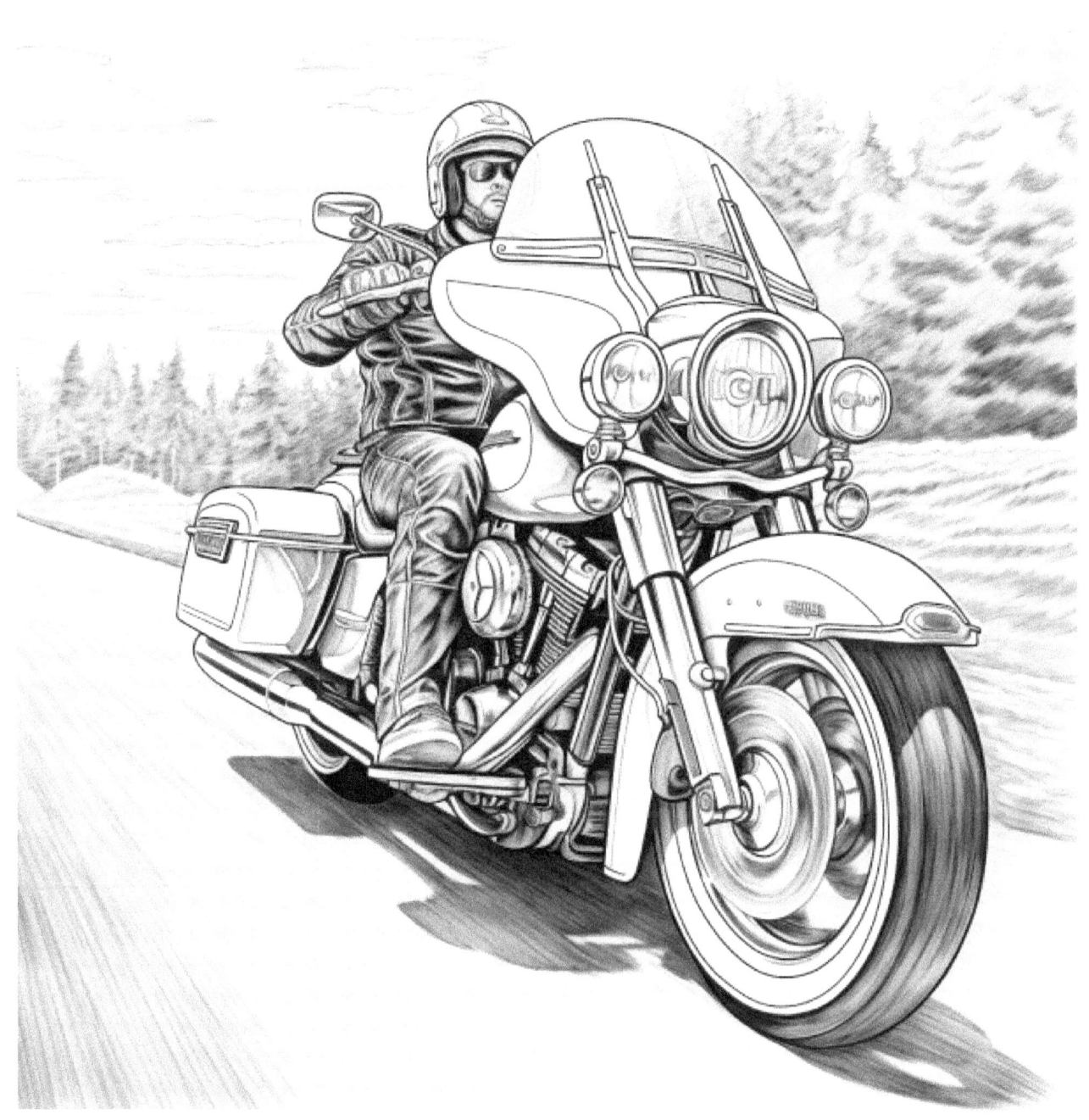

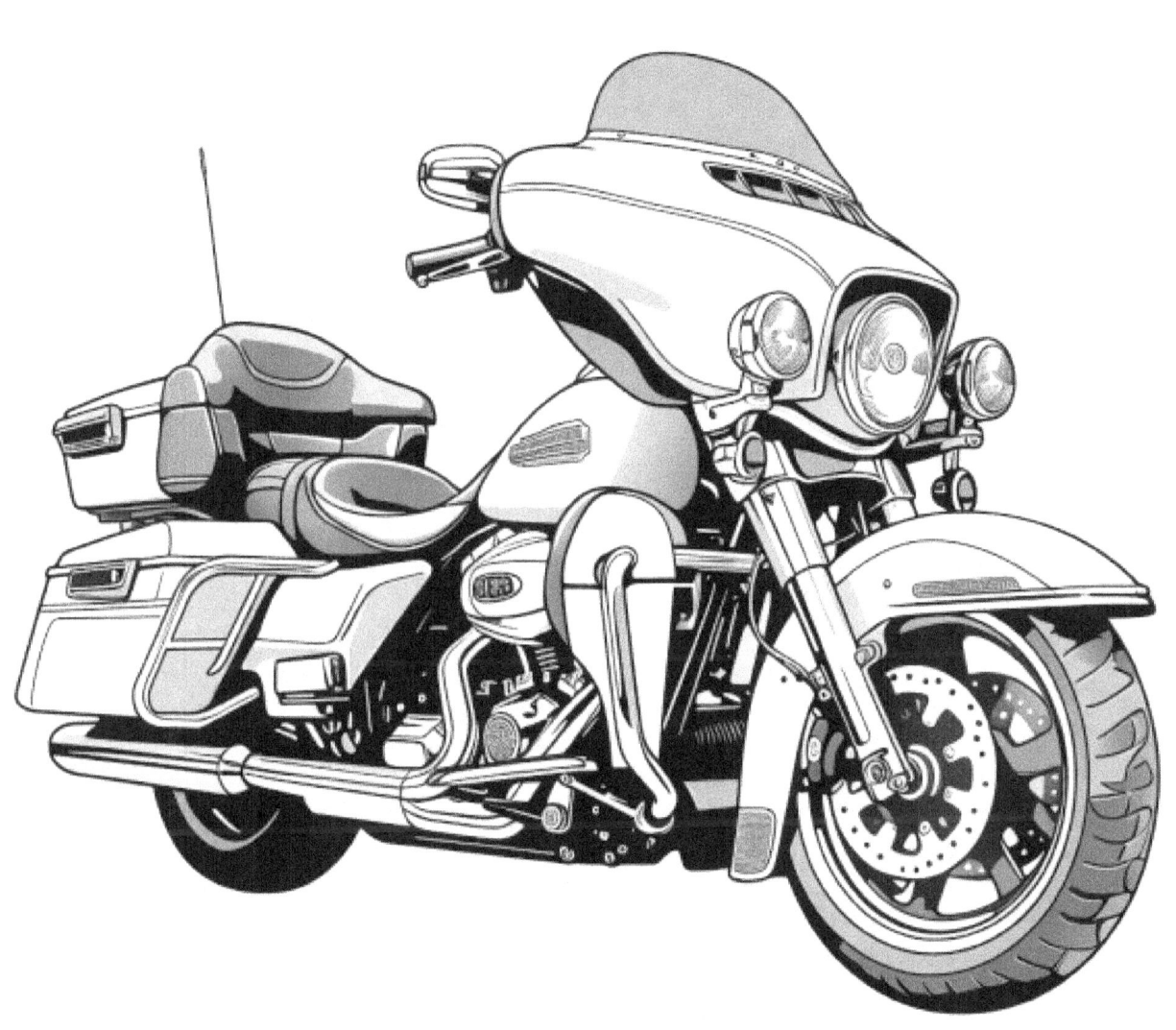

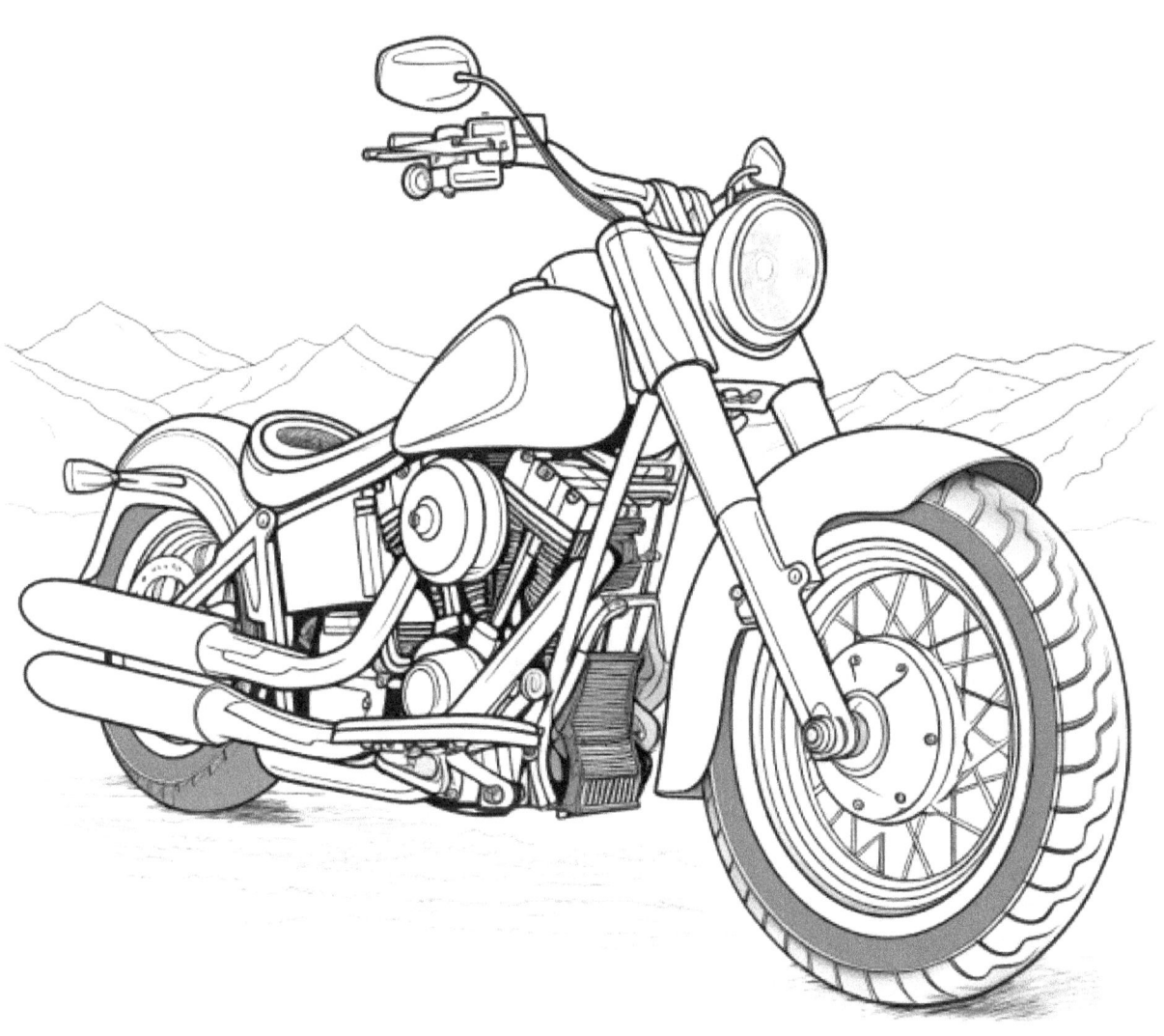

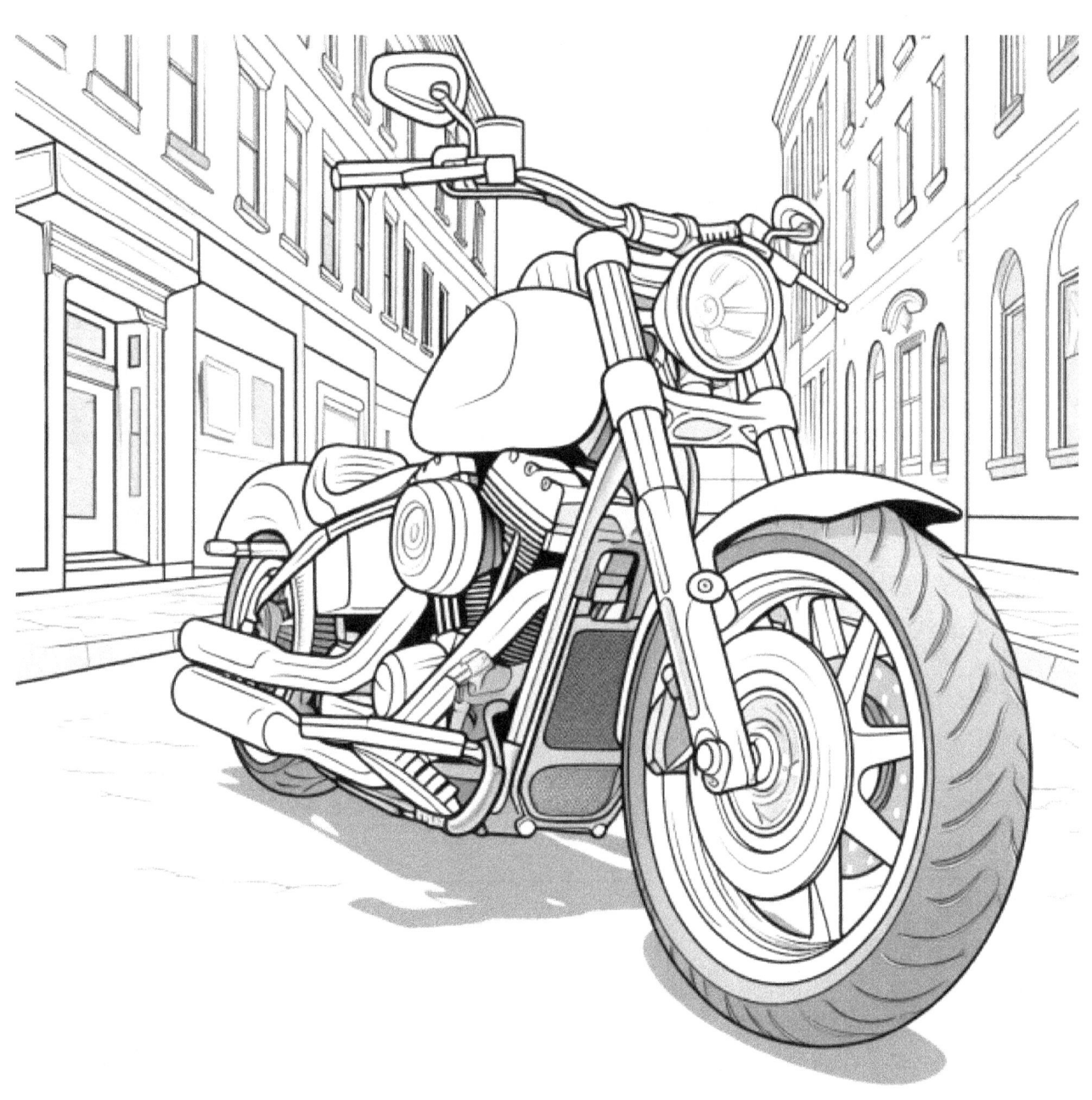

www.ingramcontent.com/pod-product-compliance
Lightning Source LLC
Chambersburg PA
CBHW082145290526
45794CB00008B/3169